Other books by Laurie Blum:

FREE MONEY FOR FOREIGN STUDY

FREE MONEY FOR GRADUATE STUDY

FREE MONEY FOR HUMANITIES STUDENTS

FREE MONEY FOR HUMANITIES & SOCIAL SCIENCES

FREE MONEY FOR MATHEMATICS & NATURAL SCIENCES

FREE MONEY FOR PEOPLE IN THE ARTS

FREE MONEY FOR PROFESSIONAL STUDIES

FREE MONEY FOR SCIENCE STUDENTS

FREE MONEY FOR SMALL BUSINESSES & ENTREPRENEURS

FREE MONEY FOR UNDERGRADUATE STUDY

HOW TO GET FEDERAL GRANTS

HOW TO INVEST IN REAL ESTATE USING FREE MONEY

Laurie Blum's

FREE MONEY

for
Day Care

A Fireside Book
Published by Simon & Schuster
New York   London   Toronto   Sydney   Tokyo   Singapore

F

FIRESIDE
Simon & Schuster Building
Rockefeller Center
1230 Avenue of the Americas
New York, New York 10020

Designed by Christina M. Riley
Manufactured in the United States of America

1 3 5 7 9 10 8 6 4 2

Library of Congress Cataloging in Publication Data
is available

ISBN 0-671-74590-5

• •

I would like to briefly but sincerely thank my "A Team," Christina, Erica, and Fori, as well as my wonderful editor Ed Walters, and of course Alan Kellock.

Contents

· · · · · · · · · · · · · · · · · · ·

Foreword

. . . .

by Susan Bernheimer
Director, Los Angeles Family School

In what way are American children cared for while their parents are at work? With so many more mothers working now, parents must deal with finding quality care for their children and yet remain as productive individuals in the work force.

Since 1976, the number of children under age six with working mothers has increased 80%. The number of children under one year old with working mothers has increased 65%. Half of the mothers with children one year old or younger are working. Today, high-quality day care begins in infancy. It is predicted that in 1995, 15 million children will be in preschool. The care of children in the home by a relative or non-relative has declined. The usage of family day care has increased, yet center care (infant care) has increased most of all. Still, half of all American children are cared for by a relative. In home day cares, 50-90% are without proper licensing. The choices of many families are constrained by their limiting income.

As a society, we have devalued childbearing and childrearing. We need to place greater importance on providing and paying for high-quality services for our children. What is happening to those children of families who cannot meet the high cost of child care? What are we as a nation doing to meet the needs of these families? We need to recruit more federal funding and corporate investments to insure the care of these children. More facilities need to open with the ability to meet the needs of a variety of income levels and cultural differences.

Free Money For Day Care is a critically needed resource. For the first time, information from government sources, foundations, and corporations is made available to parents — information about funding that will help them pay for day care expenses. Every child should have access to child care and no parent should be denied this care because of lack of adequate income. Thank you, Laurie Blum.

Introduction

In 1987, 18 million American families spent over $15 billion on day care for 29 million children under age 15. With today's firmly established realities of single-parent households and two-income families in which both parents have to (or choose to) work, the need for affordable, quality child care has become a necessity of life for most families.

While writing this book, I was amazed to discover that up until now there has been no resource guide to provide working mothers, single parents and two-income families with readily available information on existing sources of aid to help them meet the costs of their children's day care programs. I was equally shocked to learn that many employees had no idea that their own companies offered help with the costs of day care. Additionally, a number of otherwise excellent child care referral agencies with whom I spoke had no idea where to direct the middle class parent seeking assistance.

Free Money For Day Care is designed to meet this critical and ever-increasing need for information and aid by identifying thousands of sources for hundreds of thousands of dollars available to help single parents and two-income families afford the rising costs of quality child care. The quantity of information presented in this book demonstrates that there is funding assistance available to aid parents in meeting the necessary costs of day care in what for many families are recessionary and belt-tightening times. The book includes information on funding available in all fifty states and for parents at all income levels. It covers grants tied to income, as well as those with no financial strings attached.

The book is divided into five chapters:

1) "Private Foundation Funding" (listing possible sources for grants and child care subsidies);

2) "Special Population Funding" (providing information on assistance available to American Indians, Appalachian residents, parents of handicapped children, and parents of children requiring crisis care);

3) "Government Funding" (identifying agencies offering direct funding as well as essential referral information);

4) "Corporate/Employee Programs" (specifying those which provide on-site/off-site facilities and employee reimbursement programs); and

5) "Volunteer Program Funding" (identifying funding sources for community volunteer day care programs).

Within each chapter, listings are arranged state-by-state to make this book as easy to use as possible. Check your state's listings in all five chapters to see which grants or corporate programs apply to you. You'll find funding parameters and an address and phone number to contact for further information (and application forms).

By the time this book is published, some of the information contained here will have changed. No reference book can be as up-to-date as the reader or author would like. Names, addresses, dollar amounts, telephone numbers, and other data are always in flux; however, most of the information will not have changed.

While reviewing this data, readers are advised to remember that funding sources are not without restrictions and that researching, applying for, and receiving aid will take time, effort, diligence, and thought. You are going to have to identify the sources of aid for which you qualify and determine whether or not you fulfill geographic and other requirements. You are going to have to fill out applications. You may meet with rejection and frustration somewhere along this road. The odds, however, are in your favor that you will qualify for some sort of funding assistance.

Following is a concise, how-to guide to writing a grant proposal. Follow my instructions and you should be successful in obtaining some sort of day care assistance. Good luck.

How to apply

As indicated by the number of listings in this book, thousands of resources for financial aid to parents for quality child care exist throughout the country from government, private foundation, and corporate sources. Applying for this aid is the challenging part; it requires diligence, thought and organization.

First is the sorting out process or research/gathering phase. Look through each chapter of the book on a state-by-state basis (most child care funders provide aid only in their geographic area) and mark each potential assistance source. Pay close attention to the listed restrictions and qualifications, eliminating from your list the resources least likely to assist you.

Then, politely contact each of your listed sources by mail or phone to verify all current information, such as address, telephone, name of the proper contact, and his/her title (in cases where the contact's name is not listed, begin your letter, "To Whom It May Concern"). At this time, you can also arrange to get a copy of the source's most current assistance guidelines, and an application form (if that is what is required). Use this opportunity to find out about any application deadlines and to ask where you are in the funding cycle (i.e., if there is no deadline, when would be the best time to apply; also, be sure to ask when awards will be announced and funds distributed). However, never "grill" or cross-examine the person you reach on the phone. Always be prepared to talk about why you are applying and what you are applying for — in case you ring through to the key decisionmaker, who decides on the spot to interview you!

Second is the application phase. In terms of child care assistance, most often you will be asked to submit a formal
application (rather than a proposal). Usually the same
material used for one application can be applied to most, if
not all, of your other applications, with a little restructuring
(making sure you answer each and every question as asked,
appropriate to each application). Always be sure to read
(and follow!) the instructions for completing the application.

Grant applications take time (and thought) to fill out, so
make sure you give yourself enough time to do this before
the application deadline. Filling out the application can be
a lengthy process, because you may be required to write
one or more essays. Often, what is required is a "statement
of purpose" explaining what you will use the money for and
sometimes explaining why you need the assistance for
which you are applying. You may also need time to
assemble required attachments, such as tax returns and
other financial records. (Don't worry, you won't be penalized
for having money in the bank.) You may also be required to
include personal references. Be sure to get strong references. Call all of the people you plan to list, and ask them
if they feel comfortable giving you references. Remember,
you have to convince the grantors to give money to you
and not to someone else.

Be clear, concise and neat! You may very well prepare a
top-notch application, but it won't look good if it's been
prepared in a sloppy manner. Applications (and proposals)
should always be typed and double-spaced. Make sure you
keep a copy after you send off the original — I have
learned the hard way that there is nothing worse than
having the funding source be unable to find your application and your having to reconstruct it because you didn't
keep a copy.

You should apply to a number of funding sources for grants
and awards, as no one application is guaranteed to win an
award. Although none of the sources listed in this book
requires an application fee, the effort you will have to put
in will probably limit you to a maximum of eight applications (if you are ambitious and want to apply to more than
eight sources, go right ahead). Remember, the more sources
you apply to, the greater your chances for success.

The following is an example of a typical corporate/employee grant application. This one happens to be for a non-profit organization, The Parent Connection, Inc., however, the form will be similar for you as an individual and is typical of the type of grant application you will be making.

TRW Employees CHarity Organization Grant Application

To: ☒ TRW Employees Charity Organization
One Space Park, Building S, Room 1420
Redondo Beach, California 90278

☐ Other TRW ECHO Unit (Offsite)
_____
_____

Dear Grant Applicant:

Please fill in this Grant Application, providing us with the best information you have available, to aid us in evaluating your request for funds. Include, if you wish, brochures and other supporting information but any omissions on this form may prevent consideration of your request.

Thank you
TRW ECHO Governing Board

(Please Print or Type)

1. LEGAL NAME OF ORGANIZATION	FOR ECHO USE ONLY
THE PARENT CONNECTION, INC.	
2. ALSO KNOWN AS (OR FORMER NAME)	

3. ADDRESS	4. TELEPHONE NUMBER (S)
3709 SAWTELLE BLVD. LOS ANGELES, CA 90066	(213) 823-7846 ( )

5. IRS NUMBER (ATTACH CURRENT COPY OF 501(C)(3) CLEARANCE)	6. DATE ESTABLISHED
95-4115121	OCT 15, 1987

7. STAFF INFORMATION

CATEGORY	TOTAL NUMBER OF STAFF	AVERAGE HRS PER PERSON PER MONTH week	AVERAGE MONTHLY BUDGET
FULL TIME STAFF	2	40	see
PART TIME STAFF	60	4	attached
VOLUNTEERS	50	15	
BOARD MEMBERS	8	4	

8. TYPE OF SOCIAL SERVICES PROVIDED
Parental guidance classes for high-risk adult and teenage parents.

9. SUMMARIZE THE SOURCE OF ANNUAL FUNDING

FEE OR TUITIONS $	CORPORATIONS $		OTHER (SPECIFY) $
INDIVIDUALS $	*see attached* GOVERNMENT $		
UNITED WAY $	ENDOWED INCOME $		
FOUNDATIONS $			TOTAL $

10. COPY OF CURRENT BUDGET ATTACHED (IF NONE – EXPLAIN)	12. PERCENT DISTRIBUTION OF FUNDS
attached	FUND RAISING 25 %
11. COPY OF LATEST CPA AUDIT REPORT ATTACHED (IF NONE – EXPLAIN)	ADMINISTRATION 15 %
attached (1988 is not complete)	DIRECT TO SOCIAL 60 %
	100%

13. DESCRIBE THE PURPOSE FOR WHICH THE FUNDS WILL BE USED, HOW IT WILL BENEFIT A SEGMENT OF THE COMMUNITY AND DESCRIPTION OF HOW THE PROJECT WILL BE CARRIED OUT.

Funds will be used to pay for low income, underprivileged parents and teenagers to attend our SKILLFUL PARENTING: BECAUSE LOVE IS NOT ENOUGH program. We receive referrals from the dependancy and juvenile courts weekly as well as the Social Welfare Department and attorneys for parents to take the training we provide. We are instrumental in keeping families together by offering a specialized training in the fundamentals of responsible parenting. The letter they receive at the completion of the training is used in court as evidence that they have received the training. Many children are returned to parents at the completion of these classes. Enclosed is more detailed information on our classes. (The program that we offer for teenagers at Camp Scott is called "Taking Charge."

AMOUNT REQUESTED $ $5000

14. PREPARER INFORMATION

A. Jayne Major, PhD
TYPE NAME AND SIGN

Executive Director
TITLE OR POSITION

April 10, 1989
DATE

15. DESCRIBE YOUR ORGANIZATION (Include purpose, services offerred, number of people served, fee structure, chronology of accomplishments and criteria used to measure success).

1. Our purpose is to educate parents and parents to be in the most important role that they will ever have, that of raising children.

2. See attached flier for classes and for program offered at Camp Scott.

3. We serve approximately 65 people weekly in our classes. We could train more parents with financial assistance.

4. Our fee structure is $200, $150, $100 or $50 per student. Most students pay per class rather than all at once.

5. See enclosed for chronology of accomplishments.

6. Criteria used to measure success is the completion of a study guide required for letter indicating that the parent has completed the course.

16. ARE THERE OTHER CHARITIES WITH SIMILAR OR OVERLAPPING SERVICES IN YOUR AREA? IF SO, IDENTITFY.

There are other agencies that offer parent education classes. Ours is the only one where we have a continuous enrollment policy and speciallize is the most problematic of families.

17. NAMES OF TRW EMPLOYEES EITHER PARTICIPATING IN PROGRAM OR BEING SERVED.

Chuck Merriman and his wife Elissa Merriman have completed our program. Other TRW employees are invited to avail themselves of this service.

18. LIST PREVIOUS GRANTS RECEIVED FROM TRW (ECHO or corporate contributions committee) FOR 5 YEARS.

No grants have been received from TRW before.

19. ADDITIONAL COMMENTS

Thank you for the charitible work that you do, and for considering this request.

Private Foundation Funding

(includes religious funding sources)

• •

In every community, there exist private sector resources for child care assistance. This assistance is provided through private foundation funding and is generally offered in one of three forms: direct cash grants/subsidies (most often, usable only with select group providers); existing affordable day care, summer camp, after-school care, sick child care, day care for handicapped children or other programs made affordable by sliding-scale fees and subsidies; or referral services and resource programs for families who meet designated specifications.

The following sources are listed state-by-state. Please pay special attention to each listing's area of service, type and age of child served, kind of assistance offered, and any qualification restrictions. If you don't find what you need, call an appropriate source near your area or call a local source offering a different range of services — perhaps one of them can give you a helpful referral.

I also suggest that you call listings without specific service details, for more information and appropriate referral. Many nonprofit organizations offer special programs to aid clients with child care needs, but these programs are accessible only through a "grapevine" of similar service providers.

PRIVATE FOUNDATION FUNDING

• • • • • • • • • • • • • • • • • •

CALIFORNIA

Assistance League Nursery
1375 No. St. Andrews Place
Los Angeles, CA 90028
(213) 466–8164

Description: Care for children 2–6 years with parents who work or attend school; hours 7:00 a.m. to 5:30 p.m.
$ Given: Fees of $180 to $300 per month determined on sliding scale

Charo Los Angeles City Hall South
Child Development Center
111 E. First Street
Los Angeles, CA 90063
(213) 237–1267

Description: Affordable care for children (infants to age five) of city, county and federal employees; hours 6:30 a.m. to 6:00 p.m.

Child and Family Services
626 N. Colorado Terrace
Los Angeles, CA 90026
(213) 413–0777

Description: Referral service for all types of child care needs: infants, pre–school, latchkey, sick, handicapped; serves Los Angeles in downtown, Beverly Hills and Hollywood areas; hours 8:30 a.m. to 5:00 p.m.

Connections for Children
612 Colorado Avenue
Santa Monica, CA 90401
(213) 452–3202

Description: State-funded child care resource and referral program for children in West Los Angeles and South Bay; parents can call for child care information and referrals; qualified parents can go on a list for subsidized child care
$ Given: No fee for program

Crystal Stairs, Inc.
Childcare Resources &
Referrals
5105 W. Goldleaf Circle
Suite 200
Los Angeles, CA 90056
(213) 299–8998

Description: Multi–service agency including specific programs for Alternate Payment Program and Referral Program; hours 8:30 a.m. to 5:00 p.m.; serves South Central and Southwest Los Angeles; multi–ethnic
Contact: Emma Stewart

Gellert (Carl) Foundation
2222 Nineteenth Avenue
San Francisco, CA   94116
(415) 566–4420

Religious Denomination: Christian, Episcopal, Lutheran, Roman Catholic
$ Given: $1,000 to $7,500
Contact: Peter J. Brusati, Secretary

**Girls' Club of
Santa Monica**
2424 Sixth Street
Santa Monica, CA   90406
(213) 394–8433

Description: Latchkey after-school program for children 6–16 years; hours 1:00 p.m. to 6:00 p.m.
$ Given: Fee is $5.50 per year

Mervyn's
25001 Industrial Boulevard
Hayward, CA   94545
(415) 786–7492

Description: Child care
$ Given: Total: $5,858,105
Contact: Kathy Blackburn, P.A. Manager

**Moskowitz (Irving I.)
Foundation**
4201 Long Beach Blvd.
No. 304
Long Beach, CA   90807

Religious Denomination: Jewish
$ Given: $100 to $5,000
Contact: Irving I. Moskowitz, M.D.

**Stulsaft (Morris)
Foundation**
100 Bush Street
San Francisco, CA   94101
(415) 986–7117

Religious Denomination: Christian, Jewish
$ Given: $2,500 to $10,000
Contact: Joan Nelson Dills, Administrator; apply by letter to Susan Mora (6–7 month waiting period)

YWCA Los Angeles
Children's Learning Center
2519 W. Vernon Avenue
Los Angeles, CA   90008
(213) 295–4280 or 295–4288

Description: Care for children pre–school to 2 years, 9 months; before/after 6–12; hours 7:00 a.m. to 5:30 p.m.
$ Given: Fee determined on sliding scale; waived for some applicants

PRIVATE FOUNDATION FUNDING

. . . .

FLORIDA

Saint Gerard Foundation
3041 Braeloch Circle East
Clearwater, FL 34021–2708

Religious Denomination: Roman Catholic, United Methodist, Salvation Army
Contact: Elizabeth C. Mooney, Vice President

HAWAII

Teresa Hughes Trust
222 Merchant Street
Second Floor
Honolulu HI 96813
(808) 537–6333

Description: Grants to children in need, especially orphans, neglected, abused and foster children; limited to Hawaii

IDAHO

**A.P. & Louise Rouch
Boys Foundation**
c/o Twin Falls
Bank & Trust
P.O. Box 7
Twin Falls, ID 83303

Description: Assistance given for summer camp fees; relief assistance to needy children in Idaho's Magic Valley area

MARYLAND

**Mendelson (Alfred C.
& Ida) Family Foundation**
8300 Pennsylvania Avenue
P.O. Box 398
Forestville, MD 20747–0398
(301) 420–6400

Religious Denomination: Jewish
$ Given: $100 to $5,000
Contact: David Luftig, Vice President

MASSACHUSETTS

Perpetual Benefit Fund
Bay Bank Middlesex,
Trustee
300 Washington Street
Newton, MA
(617) 894–6500,
extension 5449

Description: Financial assistance for after school care for needy, one–parent families; processed through hopitals, clinics, schools, local agencies, Welfare Department
$ Given: $200 to $300

MICHIGAN

Bargman (Theodore & Mina) Foundation
29201 Telegraph Road,
Suite 500
Southfield, MI 48034
(313) 358–9500

Religious Denomination: Jewish
$ Given: $1,000 to $15,000
Contact: Lawrence Jackier, President & Trustee

W.K. Kellogg Foundation
400 North Avenue
Battle Creek, MI 49017
(619) 968–1611

$ Given: Grants vary; Total support: $106,948,094
Contact: Dr. Jack Mawdsley, Education and Youth Program Coordinator

NEW YORK

Fischel (Harry & Jane) Foundation
310 Madison Avenue,
Suite 1711
New York, NY 10001
(212) 599–2828

Religious Denomination: Jewish
$ Given: $250 to $25,000; Total: $232,568
Contact: Michael D. Jaspan, Executive Director

PRIVATE FOUNDATION FUNDING

• • • • • • • • • • • • • • • • • • • •

Wien (Lawrence A.)
Foundation, Inc.
c/o Wien, Malkin and
Bettex
60 East 42nd Street
New York, NY 10165
(212) 687–8700

Religious Denomination: Jewish, Friends, Roman
Catholic, United Methodist, Presbyterian, Protestant, and
nondenominational
$ Given: $1,000 to $6,000; Total: $703,967

NORTH CAROLINA

Stowe (Robert Lee), Jr.
Foundation, Inc.
P.O. Box 351
Belmont, NC 28012
(704) 825–5314

Religious Denomination: Roman Catholic, Presbyterian,
Baptist
$ Given: $100 to $10,000; Total: $176,644
Contact: Robert Lee Stowe III, Vice President

PENNSYLVANIA

James T. Hambay
Foundation
Dauphin Deposit Bank
& Trust Co.
P.O. Box 2961
Harrisburg, PA 17105

Description: Welfare assistance to blind, crippled, or
indigent individuals under 18; campership, day care
expenses
Application Procedure: Applications accepted throughout
year; initial approach by letter stating medical expenses
and current income
Contact: Joseph Marcri

Robert D. & Margaret W.
Quin Foundation
Hazleton National Bank
101 W. Broad Street
Hazleton, PA 18201

Description: Grants for needy students through age 19;
must have lived in 10-mile radius of Hazleton for at
least one year; pay for day care (cribs, tutoring, clothing,
etc.)
$ Given: 66 individual grants totalling $15,367

. . . .

Stern (Harry) Family Foundation
c/o Mervin J. Hartmann
Three Parkway, 20th Floor
Philadelphia, PA 19102
(215) 563–0650

Religious Denomination: Jewish
$ Given: $50 to $8,400; Total: $754,342
Contact: Jerome Stern, Secretary & Director

TENNESSEE

The Nehemiah Foundation
230 Wilson Pike Circle
P.O. Box 2036
Brentwood, TN 37027
(615) 373–1560

Description: Limited grants to parents for their children's education
Application Procedure: Applications accepted throughout the year; completion of formal application required
$ Given: Total to individuals: $16,727
Contact: William Z. Baumgartner, Jr., President

TEXAS

Ashendorf (Morris & Ann) Foundation
8323 Southwest Freeway,
Suite 300
Houston, TX 77074
(713) 270–6220

Religious Denomination: Jewish
$ Given: $500 to $13,500; Total: $72,003
Contact: H. Wesley Ashendorf

WEST VIRGINIA

Vecellio (Enrico) Family Foundation
c/o Raleigh County
National Bank, Trust Dept.
129 Main Street
P.O. Box 1269
Beckley, WV 25802
(304) 252–6581

Religious Denomination: Roman Catholic, Baptist, Methodist, Presbyterian
$ Given: $1,000 to $5,000; Total: $179,613

Special Population Funding

The following chapter on "Special Population Funding" covers day care funding assistance available to children and families in special categories. These categories include: American Indians, Appalachian residents, children requiring crisis care, and disabled children.

The category addressing funding sources for "crisis" day care is for interim day care—children requiring special kinds of crisis care on a temporary basis. It includes care for terminally/chronically ill children, abused/neglected children, and handicapped children. The national allocation of funding for crisis care for this population is $8,328,000. Local funding figures are unavailable. For national information, contact Phyllis Nophlin at (202) 245-0653.

In the final section, the national allocation of funding available for day care services to disabled children totals $82,701,000. As most parents would receive assistance through sources in their own area/region, only local contact names have been listed on a state-by-state basis. For national funding information, please contact Nancy Safer at (202) 732-1109.

SPECIAL POPULATION FUNDING

. . . .

FUNDING FOR AMERICAN INDIANS
(Only parents of qualified children may apply)

ARIZONA

Arizona Native American Training Programs
Colorado River Agency
Route 1, Box C
Parker, AZ
(602) 669-2134

Description: Funding for day care and other support services to Native Americans facing employment barriers
Amount Funded: $320,000 per tribe or Indian organization
$ Given: Variable, by need
Contact: Tribal Elder or Paul Mayrand at (202) 535-0500

Indian Child Welfare Grants for Arizona
Colorado River Agency
Route 1, Box C
Parker, AZ
(602) 669-2134

Description: Funding for family assistance, including day care and after-school care for American Indian children; provided to promote the stability of American Indian families
Amount Funded: $25,000 to over $100,000 per tribe or Indian organization
$ Given: $100+ per family
Contact: Tribal Elder or Sue Settles at (202) 343-6434

Native American Social Services Programs for Arizona
Colorado River Agency
Route 1, Box C
Parker, AZ
(602) 669-2134

Description: Free day care and after-school care for qualified American Indian children's provided as a means of improving the self-sufficiency of Native Americans
Amount Funded: $125,000 average per tribe or Indian organization
Contact: Tribal Elder or Vilma Guinn at (202) 245-7730

. . . .

CALIFORNIA

California Native American Training Programs
Central California Agency
1800 Tribute Road
P.O. Box 15740
Sacramento, CA 95813
(916) 484-4357

Description: Funding for day care and other support services to Native Americans facing employment barriers
Amount Funded: $320,000 per tribe or Indian organization
$ Given: Variable, by need
Contact: Tribal Elder or Paul Mayrand at (202) 535-0500

Indian Child Welfare Grants for California
Central California Agency
1800 Tribute Road
P.O. Box 15740
Sacramento, CA 95813
(916) 484-4357

Description: Funding for family assistance, including day care and after-school care for American Indian children; provided to promote the stability of American Indian families
Amount Funded: $25,000 to over $100,000 per tribe or Indian organization
$ Given: $100+ per family
Contact: Tribal Elder or Sue Settles at (202) 343-6434

Native American Social Services Programs for California
Central California Agency
1800 Tribute Road
P.O. Box 15740
Sacramento, CA 95813
(916) 484-4357

Description: Free day care and after-school care for qualified American Indian children's provided as a means of improving the self-sufficiency of Native Americans
Amount Funded: $125,000 average per tribe or Indian organization
Contact: Tribal Elder or Vilma Guinn at (202) 245-7730

COLORADO

Colorado Native American Training Programs
Ute Agency
Towaoc, CO 81334
(303) 565-8471

Description: Funding for day care and other support services to Native Americans facing employment barriers
Amount Funded: $320,000 per tribe or Indian organization
$ Given: Variable, by need
Contact: Tribal Elder or Paul Mayrand at (202) 535-0500

SPECIAL POPULATION FUNDING

• • • • • • • • • • • • • • • • • • •

Indian Child Welfare Grants for Colorado
Ute Agency
Towaoc, CO 81334
(303) 565-8471

Description: Funding for family assistance, including day care and after-school care for American Indian children; provided to promote the stability of American Indian families
Amount Funded: $25,000 to over $100,000 per tribe or Indian organization
$ Given: $100+ per family
Contact: Tribal Elder or Sue Settles at (202) 343-6434

Native American Social Services Programs for Colorado
Ute Agency
Towaoc, CO 81334
(303) 565-8471

Description: Free day care and after-school care for qualified American Indian children's provided as a means of improving the self-sufficiency of Native Americans
Amount Funded: $125,000 average per tribe or Indian organization
Contact: Tribal Elder or Vilma Guinn at (202) 245-7730

IOWA

Iowa Native American Training Programs
Sac and Fox Area
Field Office
Tama, IA 52339
(515) 484-4041

Description: Funding for day care and other support services to Native Americans facing employment barriers
Amount Funded: $320,000 per tribe or Indian organization
$ Given: Variable, by need
Contact: Tribal Elder or Paul Mayrand at (202) 535-0500

Indian Child Welfare Grants for Iowa
Sac and Fox Area
Field Office
Tama, IA 52339
(515) 484-4041

Description: Funding for family assistance, including day care and after-school care for American Indian children; provided to promote the stability of American Indian families
Amount Funded: $25,000 to over $100,000 per tribe or Indian organization
$ Given: $100+ per family
Contact: Tribal Elder or Sue Settles at (202) 343-6434

. . . .

**Native American Social
Services Programs for
Iowa**
Sac and Fox Area
Field Office
Tama, IA 52339
(515) 484-4041

Description: Free day care and after-school care for
qualified American Indian children's provided as a means
of improving the self-sufficiency of Native Americans
Amount Funded: $125,000 average per tribe or Indian
organization
Contact: Tribal Elder or Vilma Guinn at (202) 245-7730

KANSAS

**Kansas Native American
Training Programs**
Horton Agency
Horton, KS 66439
(913) 486-2161

Description: Funding for day care and other support
services to Native Americans facing employment barriers
Amount Funded: $320,000 per tribe or Indian organization
$ Given: Variable, by need
Contact: Tribal Elder or Paul Mayrand at (202) 535-0500

**Indian Child Welfare
Grants for Kansas**
Horton Agency
Horton, KS 66439
(913) 486-2161

Description: Funding for family assistance, including day
care and after-school care for American Indian children;
provided to promote the stability of American Indian
families
Amount Funded: $25,000 to over $100,000 per tribe or
Indian organization
$ Given: $100+ per family
Contact: Tribal Elder or Sue Settles at (202) 343-6434

**Native American Social
Services Programs for
Kansas**
Horton Agency
Horton, KS 66439
(913) 486-2161

Description: Free day care and after-school care for
qualified American Indian children's provided as a means
of improving the self-sufficiency of Native Americans
Amount Funded: $125,000 average per tribe or Indian
organization
Contact: Tribal Elder or Vilma Guinn at (202) 245-7730

SPECIAL POPULATION FUNDING

. . . .

MINNESOTA

Minnesota Native American Training Programs
Minnesota Agency
P.O. Box 97
Cass Lake, MN 56633
(218) 335-6913

Description: Funding for day care and other support services to Native Americans facing employment barriers
Amount Funded: $320,000 per tribe or Indian organization
$ Given: Variable, by need
Contact: Tribal Elder or Paul Mayrand at (202) 535-0500

Indian Child Welfare Grants for Minnesota
Minnesota Agency
P.O. Box 97
Cass Lake, MN 56633
(218) 335-6913

Description: Funding for family assistance, including day care and after-school care for American Indian children; provided to promote the stability of American Indian families
Amount Funded: $25,000 to over $100,000 per tribe or Indian organization
$ Given: $100+ per family
Contact: Tribal Elder or Sue Settles at (202) 343-6434

Native American Social Services Programs for Minnesota
Minnesota Agency
P.O. Box 97
Cass Lake, MN 56633
(218) 335-6913

Description: Free day care and after-school care for qualified American Indian children's provided as a means of improving the self-sufficiency of Native Americans
Amount Funded: $125,000 average per tribe or Indian organization
Contact: Tribal Elder or Vilma Guinn at (202) 245-7730

MONTANA

Montana Native American Training Programs
Fort Peck Agency
P.O. Box 637
Poplar, MT 59255
(406) 768-5311

Description: Funding for day care and other support services to Native Americans facing employment barriers
Amount Funded: $320,000 per tribe or Indian organization
$ Given: Variable, by need
Contact: Tribal Elder or Paul Mayrand at (202) 535-0500

Indian Child Welfare Grants for Montana
Fort Peck Agency
P.O. Box 637
Poplar, MT 59255
(406) 768-5311

Description: Funding for family assistance, including day care and after-school care for American Indian children; provided to promote the stability of American Indian families
Amount Funded: $25,000 to over $100,000 per tribe or Indian organization
$ Given: $100+ per family
Contact: Tribal Elder or Sue Settles at (202) 343-6434

Native American Social Services Programs for Montana
Fort Peck Agency
P.O. Box 637
Poplar, MT 59255
(406) 768-5311

Description: Free day care and after-school care for qualified American Indian children's provided as a means of improving the self-sufficiency of Native Americans
Amount Funded: $125,000 average per tribe or Indian organization
Contact: Tribal Elder or Vilma Guinn at (202) 245-7730

NEBRASKA

Nebraska Native American Training Programs
Winnebago Agency
Winnebago, NE 68071

Description: Funding for day care and other support services to Native Americans facing employment barriers
Amount Funded: $320,000 per tribe or Indian organization
$ Given: Variable, by need
Contact: Tribal Elder or Paul Mayrand at (202) 535-0500

Indian Child Welfare Grants for Nebraska
Winnebago Agency
Winnebago, NE 68071

Description: Funding for family assistance, including day care and after-school care for American Indian children; provided to promote the stability of American Indian families
Amount Funded: $25,000 to over $100,000 per tribe or Indian organization
$ Given: $100+ per family
Contact: Tribal Elder or Sue Settles at (202) 343-6434

. . . .

Native American Social Services Programs for Nebraska
Winnebago Agency
Winnebago, NE 68071

Description: Free day care and after-school care for qualified American Indian children's provided as a means of improving the self-sufficiency of Native Americans
Amount Funded: $125,000 average per tribe or Indian organization
Contact: Tribal Elder or Vilma Guinn at (202) 245-7730

NEVADA

Nevada Native American Training Programs
Western Nevada Agency
Stewart, NV 89437
(702) 887-3500

Description: Funding for day care and other support services to Native Americans facing employment barriers
Amount Funded: $320,000 per tribe or Indian organization
$ Given: Variable, by need
Contact: Tribal Elder or Paul Mayrand at (202) 535-0500

Indian Child Welfare Grants for Nevada
Western Nevada Agency
Stewart, NV 89437
(702) 887-3500

Description: Funding for family assistance, including day care and after-school care for American Indian children; provided to promote the stability of American Indian families
Amount Funded: $25,000 to over $100,000 per tribe or Indian organization
$ Given: $100+ per family
Contact: Tribal Elder or Sue Settles at (202) 343-6434

Native American Social Services Programs for Nevada
Western Nevada Agency
Stewart, NV 89437
(702) 887-3500

Description: Free day care and after-school care for qualified American Indian children's provided as a means of improving the self-sufficiency of Native Americans
Amount Funded: $125,000 average per tribe or Indian organization
Contact: Tribal Elder or Vilma Guinn at (202) 245-7730

• • • • • • • • • • • • • • • • • • • •

NEW MEXICO

New Mexico Native American Training Programs
Pueblos Agency
Federal Building
P.O. Box 849
Santa Fe, NM 87501
(505) 988-6431

Description: Funding for day care and other support services to Native Americans facing employment barriers
Amount Funded: $320,000 per tribe or Indian organization
$ Given: Variable, by need
Contact: Tribal Elder or Paul Mayrand at (202) 535-0500

Indian Child Welfare Grants for New Mexico
Pueblos Agency
Federal Building
P.O. Box 849
Santa Fe, NM 87501
(505) 988-6431

Description: Funding for family assistance, including day care and after-school care for American Indian children; provided to promote the stability of American Indian families
Amount Funded: $25,000 to over $100,000 per tribe or Indian organization
$ Given: $100+ per family
Contact: Tribal Elder or Sue Settles at (202) 343-6434

Native American Social Services Programs for New Mexico
Pueblos Agency
Federal Building
P.O. Box 849
Santa Fe, NM 87501
(505) 988-6431

Description: Free day care and after-school care for qualified American Indian children's provided as a means of improving the self-sufficiency of Native Americans
Amount Funded: $125,000 average per tribe or Indian organization
Contact: Tribal Elder or Vilma Guinn at (202) 245-7730

SPECIAL POPULATION FUNDING

. . . .

NEW YORK

New York Native American Training Programs
New York Field Office
Federal Building, No 523
100 South Clinton Street
Syracuse, NY 13202
(315) 423-5476

Description: Funding for day care and other support services to Native Americans facing employment barriers
Amount Funded: $320,000 per tribe or Indian organization
$ Given: Variable, by need
Contact: Tribal Elder or Paul Mayrand at (202) 535-0500

Indian Child Welfare Grants for New York
New York Field Office
Federal Building, No 523
100 South Clinton Street
Syracuse, NY 13202
(315) 423-5476

Description: Funding for family assistance, including day care and after-school care for American Indian children; provided to promote the stability of American Indian families
Amount Funded: $25,000 to over $100,000 per tribe or Indian organization
$ Given: $100+ per family
Contact: Tribal Elder or Sue Settles at (202) 343-6434

Native American Social Services Programs for New York
New York Field Office
Federal Building, No 523
100 South Clinton Street
Syracuse, NY 13202
(315) 423-5476

Description: Free day care and after-school care for qualified American Indian children's provided as a means of improving the self-sufficiency of Native Americans
Amount Funded: $125,000 average per tribe or Indian organization
Contact: Tribal Elder or Vilma Guinn at (202) 245-7730

NORTH CAROLINA

North Carolina Native American Training Programs
Cherokee Agency
Cherokee, NC 28719
(704) 497-9131

Description: Funding for day care and other support services to Native Americans facing employment barriers
Amount Funded: $320,000 per tribe or Indian organization
$ Given: Variable, by need
Contact: Tribal Elder or Paul Mayrand at (202) 535-0500

• •

Indian Child Welfare Grants for North Carolina
Cherokee Agency
Cherokee, NC 28719
(704) 497-9131

Description: Funding for family assistance, including day care and after-school care for American Indian children; provided to promote the stability of American Indian families
Amount Funded: $25,000 to over $100,000 per tribe or Indian organization
$ Given: $100+ per family
Contact: Tribal Elder or Sue Settles at (202) 343-6434

Native American Social Services Programs for North Carolina
Cherokee Agency
Cherokee, NC 28719
(704) 497-9131

Description: Free day care and after-school care for qualified American Indian children's provided as a means of improving the self-sufficiency of Native Americans
Amount Funded: $125,000 average per tribe or Indian organization
Contact: Tribal Elder or Vilma Guinn at (202) 245-7730

NORTH DAKOTA

North Dakota Native American Training Programs
Turtle Mountain Agency
Belcourt, ND 58316
(701) 477-3191

Description: Funding for day care and other support services to Native Americans facing employment barriers
Amount Funded: $320,000 per tribe or Indian organization
$ Given: Variable, by need
Contact: Tribal Elder or Paul Mayrand at (202) 535-0500

Indian Child Welfare Grants for North Dakota
Turtle Mountain Agency
Belcourt, ND 58316
(701) 477-3191

Description: Funding for family assistance, including day care and after-school care for American Indian children; provided to promote the stability of American Indian families
Amount Funded: $25,000 to over $100,000 per tribe or Indian organization
$ Given: $100+ per family
Contact: Tribal Elder or Sue Settles at (202) 343-6434

SPECIAL POPULATION FUNDING

• • • • • • • • • • • • • • • • • • • •

Native American Social Services Programs for North Dakota
Turtle Mountain Agency
Belcourt, ND 58316
(701) 477-3191

Description: Free day care and after-school care for qualified American Indian children's provided as a means of improving the self-sufficiency of Native Americans
Amount Funded: $125,000 average per tribe or Indian organization
Contact: Tribal Elder or Vilma Guinn at (202) 245-7730

OKLAHOMA

Oklahoma Native American Training Programs
Pawnee Agency
P.O. Box 440
Pawnee, OK 74058
(918) 762-2585

Description: Funding for day care and other support services to Native Americans facing employment barriers
Amount Funded: $320,000 per tribe or Indian organization
$ Given: Variable, by need
Contact: Tribal Elder or Paul Mayrand at (202) 535-0500

Indian Child Welfare Grants for Oklahoma
Pawnee Agency
P.O. Box 440
Pawnee, OK 74058
(918) 762-2585

Description: Funding for family assistance, including day care and after-school care for American Indian children; provided to promote the stability of American Indian families
Amount Funded: $25,000 to over $100,000 per tribe or Indian organization
$ Given: $100+ per family
Contact: Tribal Elder or Sue Settles at (202) 343-6434

Native American Social Services Programs for Oklahoma
Pawnee Agency
P.O. Box 440
Pawnee, OK 74058
(918) 762-2585

Description: Free day care and after-school care for qualified American Indian children's provided as a means of improving the self-sufficiency of Native Americans
Amount Funded: $125,000 average per tribe or Indian organization
Contact: Tribal Elder or Vilma Guinn at (202) 245-7730

OREGON

Oregon Native American Training Programs
Warm Springs Agency
Warm Springs, OR 97761
(503) 553-1121

Description: Funding for day care and other support services to Native Americans facing employment barriers
Amount Funded: $320,000 per tribe or Indian organization
$ Given: Variable, by need
Contact: Tribal Elder or Paul Mayrand at (202) 535-0500

Indian Child Welfare Grants for Oregon
Warm Springs Agency
Warm Springs, OR 97761
(503) 553-1121

Description: Funding for family assistance, including day care and after-school care for American Indian children; provided to promote the stability of American Indian families
Amount Funded: $25,000 to over $100,000 per tribe or Indian organization
$ Given: $100+ per family
Contact: Tribal Elder or Sue Settles at (202) 343-6434

Native American Social Services Programs for Oregon
Warm Springs Agency
Warm Springs, OR 97761
(503) 553-1121

Description: Free day care and after-school care for qualified American Indian children's provided as a means of improving the self-sufficiency of Native Americans
Amount Funded: $125,000 average per tribe or Indian organization
Contact: Tribal Elder or Vilma Guinn at (202) 245-7730

SOUTH DAKOTA

South Dakota Native American Training Programs
Cheyenne River Agency
P.O. Box 325
Eagle Butte, SD 57625
(605) 964-6611

Description: Funding for day care and other support services to Native Americans facing employment barriers
Amount Funded: $320,000 per tribe or Indian organization
$ Given: Variable, by need
Contact: Tribal Elder or Paul Mayrand at (202) 535-0500

SPECIAL POPULATION FUNDING

• • • • • • • • • • • • • • • • • • • •

Indian Child Welfare Grants for South Dakota
Cheyenne River Agency
P.O. Box 325
Eagle Butte, SD 57625
(605) 964-6611

Description: Funding for family assistance, including day care and after-school care for American Indian children; provided to promote the stability of American Indian families
Amount Funded: $25,000 to over $100,000 per tribe or Indian organization
$ Given: $100+ per family
Contact: Tribal Elder or Sue Settles at (202) 343-6434

Native American Social Services Programs for South Dakota
Cheyenne River Agency
P.O. Box 325
Eagle Butte, SD 57625
(605) 964-6611

Description: Free day care and after-school care for qualified American Indian children's provided as a means of improving the self-sufficiency of Native Americans
Amount Funded: $125,000 average per tribe or Indian organization
Contact: Tribal Elder or Vilma Guinn at (202) 245-7730

UTAH

Utah Native American Training Programs
Uintah and Ouray Agency
Fort Duchense, UT 84026
(801) 722-2406

Description: Funding for day care and other support services to Native Americans facing employment barriers
Amount Funded: $320,000 per tribe or Indian organization
$ Given: Variable, by need
Contact: Tribal Elder or Paul Mayrand at (202) 535-0500

Indian Child Welfare Grants for Utah
Uintah and Ouray Agency
Fort Duchense, UT 84026
(801) 722-2406

Description: Funding for family assistance, including day care and after-school care for American Indian children; provided to promote the stability of American Indian families
Amount Funded: $25,000 to over $100,000 per tribe or Indian organization
$ Given: $100+ per family
Contact: Tribal Elder or Sue Settles at (202) 343-6434

• • • • • • • • • • • • • • • • • • • •

**Native American Social
Services Programs for
Utah**
Uintah and Ouray Agency
Fort Duchense, UT 84026
(801) 722-2406

Description: Free day care and after-school care for
qualified American Indian children's provided as a means
of improving the self-sufficiency of Native Americans
Amount Funded: $125,000 average per tribe or Indian
organization
Contact: Tribal Elder or Vilma Guinn at (202) 245-7730

WASHINGTON

**Washington Native
American Training
Programs**
Puget Sound Agency
3006 Colby Avenue
Federal Building
Everett, WA 98201
(206) 258-2651

Description: Funding for day care and other support
services to Native Americans facing employment barriers
Amount Funded: $320,000 per tribe or Indian organization
$ Given: Variable, by need
Contact: Tribal Elder or Paul Mayrand at (202) 535-0500

**Indian Child Welfare
Grants for Washington**
Puget Sound Agency
3006 Colby Avenue
Federal Building
Everett, WA 98201
(206) 258-2651

Description: Funding for family assistance, including day
care and after-school care for American Indian children;
provided to promote the stability of American Indian
families
Amount Funded: $25,000 to over $100,000 per tribe or
Indian organization
$ Given: $100+ per family
Contact: Tribal Elder or Sue Settles at (202) 343-6434

**Native American Social
Services Programs for
Washington**
Puget Sound Agency
3006 Colby Avenue
Federal Building
Everett, WA 98201
(206) 258-2651

Description: Free day care and after-school care for
qualified American Indian children's provided as a means
of improving the self-sufficiency of Native Americans
Amount Funded: $125,000 average per tribe or Indian
organization
Contact: Tribal Elder or Vilma Guinn at (202) 245-7730

SPECIAL POPULATION FUNDING

. . . .

WISCONSIN

Wisconsin Native American Training Programs
Great Lakes Agency
Ashland, WI 54806
(715) 682-4527

Description: Funding for day care and other support services to Native Americans facing employment barriers
Amount Funded: $320,000 per tribe or Indian organization
$ Given: Variable, by need
Contact: Tribal Elder or Paul Mayrand at (202) 535-0500

Indian Child Welfare Grants for Wisconsin
Great Lakes Agency
Ashland, WI 54806
(715) 682-4527

Description: Funding for family assistance, including day care and after-school care for American Indian children; provided to promote the stability of American Indian families
Amount Funded: $25,000 to over $100,000 per tribe or Indian organization
$ Given: $100+ per family
Contact: Tribal Elder or Sue Settles at (202) 343-6434

Native American Social Services Programs for Wisconsin
Great Lakes Agency
Ashland, WI 54806
(715) 682-4527

Description: Free day care and after-school care for qualified American Indian children's provided as a means of improving the self-sufficiency of Native Americans
Amount Funded: $125,000 average per tribe or Indian organization
Contact: Tribal Elder or Vilma Guinn at (202) 245-7730

WYOMING

Wyoming Native American Training Programs
Wind River Agency
Fort Washakie, WY 82514
(307) 225-8301

Description: Funding for day care and other support services to Native Americans facing employment barriers
Amount Funded: $320,000 per tribe or Indian organization
$ Given: Variable, by need
Contact: Tribal Elder or Paul Mayrand at (202) 535-0500

Indian Child Welfare Grants for Wyoming
Wind River Agency
Fort Washakie, WY 82514
(307) 225-8301

Description: Funding for family assistance, including day care and after-school care for American Indian children; provided to promote the stability of American Indian families
Amount Funded: $25,000 to over $100,000 per tribe or Indian organization
$ Given: $100+ per family
Contact: Tribal Elder or Sue Settles at (202) 343-6434

Native American Social Services Programs for Wyoming
Wind River Agency
Fort Washakie, WY 82514
(307) 225-8301

Description: Free day care and after-school care for qualified American Indian children's provided as a means of improving the self-sufficiency of Native Americans
Amount Funded: $125,000 average per tribe or Indian organization
Contact: Tribal Elder or Vilma Guinn at (202) 245-7730

SPECIAL POPULATION FUNDING

• • • • • • • • • • • • • • • • • • • •

FUNDING FOR APPALACHIAN RESIDENTS
(Only parents of children up to 6 years old may apply)

ALABAMA

Alabama Appalachian Vocational and Other Educational Grants
Department of Economic and Community Affairs
Box 250347, 3465 Norman Bridge Road
Montgomery, AL 36125
(205) 242-8672

Description: Funding for child care and development services in Appalachia
Average Amount Funded: $34,870 per organization
$ Given: $300 to $1,500 per family
Contact: Director

GEORGIA

Georgia Appalachian Vocational and Other Educational Grants
1200 Equitable Building
100 Peachtree Street
Atlanta, GA 30303
(404) 656-3836

Description: Funding for child care and development services in Appalachia
Average Amount Funded: $34,870 per organization
$ Given: $300 to $1,500 per family
Contact: Director

KENTUCKY

Kentucky Appalachian Vocational and Other Educational Grants
Capital Tower Plaza
Frankfort, KY 40601
(502) 564-2382

Description: Funding for child care and development services in Appalachia
Average Amount Funded: $34,870 per organization
$ Given: $300 to $1,500 per family
Contact: Director

MARYLAND

Maryland Appalachian Vocational and Other Educational Grants
301 West Preston Street, Room 1101
Annapolis, MD 21201
(301) 255-4510

Description: Funding for child care and development services in Appalachia
Average Amount Funded: $34,870 per organization
$ Given: $300 to $1,500 per family
Contact: Director

MISSISSIPPI

Mississippi Appalachian Vocational and Other Educational Grants
State Office of Appalachia
Box 1606
Tupelo, MS 38802
(601) 844-1184

Description: Funding for child care and development services in Appalachia
Average Amount Funded: $34,870 per organization
$ Given: $300 to $1,500 per family
Contact: Director

NEW YORK

New York Appalachian Vocational and Other Educational Grants
Department of State
162 Washington Avenue
Albany, NY 12231
(518) 474-4750

Description: Funding for child care and development services in Appalachia
Average Amount Funded: $34,870 per organization
$ Given: $300 to $1,500 per family
Contact: Director

NORTH CAROLINA

North Carolina Appalachian Vocational and Other Educational Grants
Dept. of Administration
116 West Jones Street
Raleigh, NC 27611
(919) 733-7232

Description: Funding for child care and development services in Appalachia
Average Amount Funded: $34,870 per organization
$ Given: $300 to $1,500 per family
Contact: Director

SPECIAL POPULATION FUNDING

· ·

OHIO

Ohio Appalachian Vocational and Other Educational Grants
Governor's Office of
Appalachia
77 South High Street
Columbus, OH 43266
(614) 644-9228

Description: Funding for child care and development services in Appalachia
Average Amount Funded: $34,870 per organization
$ Given: $300 to $1,500 per family
Contact: Director

PENNSYLVANIA

Pennsylvania Appalachian Vocational and Other Educational Grants
Department of Commerce
Forum Building, Room 433
Harrisburg, PA 17120
(717) 787-3003

Description: Funding for child care and development services in Appalachia
Average Amount Funded: $34,870 per organization
$ Given: $300 to $1,500 per family
Contact: Director

SOUTH CAROLINA

South Carolina Appalachian Vocational and Other Educational Grants
Office of the Governor
444 North Capitol Street,
Suite 234
Washington, DC 20001
(202) 624-7784

Description: Funding for child care and development services in Appalachia
Average Amount Funded: $34,870 per organization
$ Given: $300 to $1,500 per family
Contact: Director

• •

TENNESSEE

Tennessee Appalachian Vocational and Other Educational Grants
Community Development Division
320 Sixth Avenue, North
Nashville, TN 37219
(615) 741-2373

Description: Funding for child care and development services in Appalachia
Average Amount Funded: $34,870 per organization
$ Given: $300 to $1,500 per family
Contact: Director

VIRGINIA

Virginia Appalachian Vocational and Other Educational Grants
Department of Housing and Community Development
205 North Fourth Street
Richmond, VA 23219
(804) 786-1575

Description: Funding for child care and development services in Appalachia
Average Amount Funded: $34,870 per organization
$ Given: $300 to $1,500 per family
Contact: Director

WEST VIRGINIA

West Virginia Appalachian Vocational and Other Educational Grants
Governor's Office of Community and Industrial Development
Building 1, Room M-146
State Capitol Complex
Charleston, WV 25305
(304) 348-0400

Description: Funding for child care and development services in Appalachia
Average Amount Funded: $34,870 per organization
$ Given: $300 to $1,500 per family
Contact: Director

SPECIAL POPULATION FUNDING

· ·

SERVICES FOR CHILDREN REQUIRING CRISIS CARE
(Individuals may apply through state agencies)

ALABAMA

Temporary Child Care and Crisis Nurseries in Alabama
Department of Health and Social Services
434 Monroe Street,
Room 381
Montgomery, AL 36130
(205) 261-5052

Description: New program providing temporary non-medical care for handicapped children, children with chronic or terminal illnesses, and abused or neglected children; designed to alleviate social, emotional and financial stress among their families
$ Given: Undetermined
Contact: Claude Fox

ALASKA

Temporary Child Care and Crisis Nurseries in Alaska
Department of Health and Social Services
350 Main Street
Juneau, AK 99822
(907) 465-3030

Description: New program providing temporary non-medical care for handicapped children, children with chronic or terminal illnesses, and abused or neglected children; designed to alleviate social, emotional and financial stress among their families
$ Given: Undetermined
Contact: Myra Munson

ARIZONA

Temporary Child Care and Crisis Nurseries in Arizona
Department of Health and Social Services
1740 West Adams Street
Phoenix, AZ 85007
(602) 542-1024

Description: New program providing temporary non-medical care for handicapped children, children with chronic or terminal illnesses, and abused or neglected children; designed to alleviate social, emotional and financial stress among their families
$ Given: Undetermined
Contact: Ted Williams

• • • • • • • • • • • • • • • • •

ARKANSAS

Temporary Child Care and Crisis Nurseries in Arkansas
Department Health and Social Services
4815 West Markham Street
Little Rock, AR 72205
(501) 661-2242

Description: New program providing temporary non-medical care for handicapped children, children with chronic or terminal illnesses, and abused or neglected children; designed to alleviate social, emotional and financial stress among their families
$ Given: Undetermined
Contact: M. Jocelyn Elders

CALIFORNIA

Temporary Child Care and Crisis Nurseries in California
Department of Health and Social Services
714 P Street, Room 1253
Sacramento, CA 95814
(916) 445-1248

Description: New program providing temporary non-medical care for handicapped children, children with chronic or terminal illnesses, and abused or neglected children; designed to alleviate social, emotional and financial stress among their families
$ Given: Undetermined
Contact: Kenneth Kizer

COLORADO

Temporary Child Care and Crisis Nurseries in Colorado
Department of Health and Social Services
4210 East 11th
Denver, CO 80220
(303) 331-4510

Description: New program providing temporary non-medical care for handicapped children, children with chronic or terminal illnesses, and abused or neglected children; designed to alleviate social, emotional and financial stress among their families
$ Given: Undetermined
Contact: Thomas Vernon

SPECIAL POPULATION FUNDING

. . . .

CONNECTICUT

**Temporary Child Care
and Crisis Nurseries in
Connecticut**
Department of Health and
Social Services
150 Washington Street
Hartford, CT 06106
(203) 566-2038

Description: New program providing temporary non-medical care for handicapped children, children with chronic or terminal illnesses, and abused or neglected children; designed to alleviate social, emotional and financial stress among their families
$ Given: Undetermined
Contact: Fredrick Adams

DELAWARE

**Temporary Child Care
and Crisis Nurseries in
Delaware**
Department of Health and
Social Services
P.O. Box 637
Dover, DE 19903
(302) 736-4701

Description: New program providing temporary non-medical care for handicapped children, children with chronic or terminal illnesses, and abused or neglected children; designed to alleviate social, emotional and financial stress among their families
$ Given: Undetermined
Contact: Lyman Olsen

FLORIDA

**Temporary Child Care
and Crisis Nurseries in
Florida**
Department of Health and
Social Services
1323 Winewood Road,
Room 115
Tallahassee, FL 32399
(904) 487-2705

Description: New program providing temporary non-medical care for handicapped children, children with chronic or terminal illnesses, and abused or neglected children; designed to alleviate social, emotional and financial stress among their families
$ Given: Undetermined
Contact: Charles Mahan

GEORGIA

Temporary Child Care and Crisis Nurseries in Georgia
Department of Health and Social Services
878 Peachtree Street, NE, Suite 201
Atlanta, GA 30309
(404) 894-7505

Description: New program providing temporary non-medical care for handicapped children, children with chronic or terminal illnesses, and abused or neglected children; designed to alleviate social, emotional and financial stress among their families
$ Given: Undetermined
Contact: James Alley

HAWAII

Temporary Child Care and Crisis Nurseries in Hawaii
Department of Health and Social Services
P.O. Box 3378
Honolulu, HI 96801
(808) 548-6505

Description: New program providing temporary non-medical care for handicapped children, children with chronic or terminal illnesses, and abused or neglected children; designed to alleviate social, emotional and financial stress among their families
$ Given: Undetermined
Contact: John C. Lewin

IDAHO

Temporary Child Care and Crisis Nurseries in Idaho
Department of Health and Social Services
450 West State Street, 4th Floor
Boise, ID 83720
(208) 334-5930

Description: New program providing temporary non-medical care for handicapped children, children with chronic or terminal illnesses, and abused or neglected children; designed to alleviate social, emotional and financial stress among their families
$ Given: Undetermined
Contact: Fritz Dixon

SPECIAL POPULATION FUNDING

. . . .

ILLINOIS

Temporary Child Care and Crisis Nurseries in Illinois
Department of Health and Social Services
535 West Jefferson Street
Springfield, IL 62761
(217) 782-4977

Description: New program providing temporary non-medical care for handicapped children, children with chronic or terminal illnesses, and abused or neglected children; designed to alleviate social, emotional and financial stress among their families
$ Given: Undetermined
Contact: Bernard Turnock

INDIANA

Temporary Child Care and Crisis Nurseries in Indiana
Department of Health and Social Services
1330 West Michigan Street
Indianapolis, IN 46206
(317) 633-8400

Description: New program providing temporary non-medical care for handicapped children, children with chronic or terminal illnesses, and abused or neglected children; designed to alleviate social, emotional and financial stress among their families
$ Given: Undetermined
Contact: Woodrow Myers

IOWA

Temporary Child Care and Crisis Nurseries in Iowa
Department of Health and Social Services
East 12th & Walnut Streets
Des Moines, IA 50319
(515) 281-5605

Description: New program providing temporary non-medical care for handicapped children, children with chronic or terminal illnesses, and abused or neglected children; designed to alleviate social, emotional and financial stress among their families
$ Given: Undetermined
Contact: Mary Ellis

KANSAS

Temporary Child Care and Crisis Nurseries in Kansas
Department of Health and Social Services
900 SW Jackson
Topeka, KS 66612
(913) 296-1343

Description: New program providing temporary non-medical care for handicapped children, children with chronic or terminal illnesses, and abused or neglected children; designed to alleviate social, emotional and financial stress among their families
$ Given: Undetermined
Contact: Charles Konigsberg

KENTUCKY

Temporary Child Care and Crisis Nurseries in Kentucky
Department of Health and Social Services
275 East Main Street, First Floor
Frankfort, KY 40601
(502) 564-4770

Description: New program providing temporary non-medical care for handicapped children, children with chronic or terminal illnesses, and abused or neglected children; designed to alleviate social, emotional and financial stress among their families
$ Given: Undetermined
Contact: Carlos Hernandez

LOUISIANA

Temporary Child Care and Crisis Nurseries in Louisiana
Department of Health and Social Services
P.O. Box 60630
Baton Rouge, LA 70160
(504) 568-5051

Description: New program providing temporary non-medical care for handicapped children, children with chronic or terminal illnesses, and abused or neglected children; designed to alleviate social, emotional and financial stress among their families
$ Given: Undetermined
Contact: Carlos Carbo

SPECIAL POPULATION FUNDING

• • • • • • • • • • • • • • • • • • • •

MAINE

Temporary Child Care and Crisis Nurseries in Maine
Department of Health and Social Services
151 Capitol Street
Augusta, ME 04333
(207) 289-3201

Description: New program providing temporary non-medical care for handicapped children, children with chronic or terminal illnesses, and abused or neglected children; designed to alleviate social, emotional and financial stress among their families
$ Given: Undetermined
Contact: Helen Zidowecki

MARYLAND

Temporary Child Care and Crisis Nurseries in Maryland
Department of Health and Social Services
201 Preston Street
Baltimore, MD 21201
(301) 225-6500

Description: New program providing temporary non-medical care for handicapped children, children with chronic or terminal illnesses, and abused or neglected children; designed to alleviate social, emotional and financial stress among their families
$ Given: Undetermined
Contact: Adele Wilzack

MASSACHUSETTS

Temporary Child Care and Crisis Nurseries in Massachusetts
Department of Health and Social Services
150 Tremont Street
Boston, MA 02111
(617) 727-0201

Description: New program providing temporary non-medical care for handicapped children, children with chronic or terminal illnesses, and abused or neglected children; designed to alleviate social, emotional and financial stress among their families
$ Given: Undetermined
Contact: Deborah Prothrow-Stith

• •

MICHIGAN

Temporary Child Care and Crisis Nurseries in Michigan
Department of Health and Social Services
P.O. Box 30195
Lansing, MI 48909
(517) 335-8024

Description: New program providing temporary non-medical care for handicapped children, children with chronic or terminal illnesses, and abused or neglected children; designed to alleviate social, emotional and financial stress among their families
$ Given: Undetermined
Contact: Raj Weiner

MINNESOTA

Temporary Child Care and Crisis Nurseries in Minnesota
Department of Health and Social Services
717 Delaware Street, SE, Room 262
Minneapolis, MN 55440
(612) 623-5460

Description: New program providing temporary non-medical care for handicapped children, children with chronic or terminal illnesses, and abused or neglected children; designed to alleviate social, emotional and financial stress among their families
$ Given: Undetermined
Contact: Mary Ashton

MISSISSIPPI

Temporary Child Care and Crisis Nurseries in Mississippi
Department of Health and Social Services
2423 North State Street
Jackson, MS 39215
(601) 960-7634

Description: New program providing temporary non-medical care for handicapped children, children with chronic or terminal illnesses, and abused or neglected children; designed to alleviate social, emotional and financial stress among their families
$ Given: Undetermined
Contact: Alton Cobb

SPECIAL POPULATION FUNDING

· ·

MISSOURI

Temporary Child Care and Crisis Nurseries in Missouri
Department of Health and Social Services
P.O. Box 570
Jefferson City, MO 65102
(314) 751-6002

Description: New program providing temporary non-medical care for handicapped children, children with chronic or terminal illnesses, and abused or neglected children; designed to alleviate social, emotional and financial stress among their families
$ Given: Undetermined
Contact: Robert Harmon

MONTANA

Temporary Child Care and Crisis Nurseries in Montana
Department of Health and Social Services
Cogswell Building, Room C108
Helena, MT 59620
(406) 444-2544

Description: New program providing temporary non-medical care for handicapped children, children with chronic or terminal illnesses, and abused or neglected children; designed to alleviate social, emotional and financial stress among their families
$ Given: Undetermined
Contact: John Drynan

NEBRASKA

Temporary Child Care and Crisis Nurseries in Nebraska
Department of Health and Social Services
301 Centennial Mall, South
Lincoln, NE 68509
(402) 471-2133

Description: New program providing temporary non-medical care for handicapped children, children with chronic or terminal illnesses, and abused or neglected children; designed to alleviate social, emotional and financial stress among their families
$ Given: Undetermined
Contact: Gregg Wright

NEVADA

Temporary Child Care and Crisis Nurseries in Nevada
Department of Health and Social Services
505 East King Street
Carson City, NV 89710
(702) 885-4740

Description: New program providing temporary non-medical care for handicapped children, children with chronic or terminal illnesses, and abused or neglected children; designed to alleviate social, emotional and financial stress among their families
$ Given: Undetermined
Contact: Joseph Q. Jarvis

NEW HAMPSHIRE

Temporary Child Care and Crisis Nurseries in New Hampshire
Department of Health and Social Services
6 Hazen Drive
Concord, NH 03301
(603) 271-4501

Description: New program providing temporary non-medical care for handicapped children, children with chronic or terminal illnesses, and abused or neglected children; designed to alleviate social, emotional and financial stress among their families
$ Given: Undetermined
Contact: William T. Wallace

NEW JERSEY

Temporary Child Care and Crisis Nurseries in New Jersey
Department of Health and Social Services
CN 360
Trenton, NJ 08625
(609) 292-7837

Description: New program providing temporary non-medical care for handicapped children, children with chronic or terminal illnesses, and abused or neglected children; designed to alleviate social, emotional and financial stress among their families
$ Given: Undetermined
Contact: Molly Joel Coye

SPECIAL POPULATION FUNDING

. . . .

NEW MEXICO

Temporary Child Care and Crisis Nurseries in New Mexico
Department of Health and Social Services
1190 St. Francis Drive
Santa Fe, NM 87504
(505) 827-0020

Description: New program providing temporary non-medical care for handicapped children, children with chronic or terminal illnesses, and abused or neglected children; designed to alleviate social, emotional and financial stress among their families
$ Given: Undetermined
Contact: Roy McKeag

NEW YORK

Temporary Child Care and Crisis Nurseries in New York
Department of Health and Social Services
Corning Tower, Room 1408
Albany, NY 12237
(518) 474-2011

Description: New program providing temporary non-medical care for handicapped children, children with chronic or terminal illnesses, and abused or neglected children; designed to alleviate social, emotional and financial stress among their families
$ Given: Undetermined
Contact: David Axelrod

NORTH CAROLINA

Temporary Child Care and Crisis Nurseries in North Carolina
Department of Health and Social Services
225 North McDowell Street
Raleigh, NC 27602
(919) 733-3446

Description: New program providing temporary non-medical care for handicapped children, children with chronic or terminal illnesses, and abused or neglected children; designed to alleviate social, emotional and financial stress among their families
$ Given: Undetermined
Contact: Ronald Levine

NORTH DAKOTA

Temporary Child Care and Crisis Nurseries in North Dakota
Department of Health and Social Services
State Capitol
Bismarck, ND 58505
(701) 224-2372

Description: New program providing temporary non-medical care for handicapped children, children with chronic or terminal illnesses, and abused or neglected children; designed to alleviate social, emotional and financial stress among their families
$ Given: Undetermined
Contact: Robert Wentz

OHIO

Temporary Child Care and Crisis Nurseries in Ohio
Department of Health and Social Services
246 North High Street
Columbus, OH 43226
(614) 466-3543

Description: New program providing temporary non-medical care for handicapped children, children with chronic or terminal illnesses, and abused or neglected children; designed to alleviate social, emotional and financial stress among their families
$ Given: Undetermined
Contact: Ronald Fletcher

OKLAHOMA

Temporary Child Care and Crisis Nurseries in Oklahoma
Department of Health and Social Services
100 NE 10th Street
Oklahoma City, OK 73152
(405) 271-4200

Description: New program providing temporary non-medical care for handicapped children, children with chronic or terminal illnesses, and abused or neglected children; designed to alleviate social, emotional and financial stress among their families
$ Given: Undetermined
Contact: Joan Leavitt

SPECIAL POPULATION FUNDING

. . . .

OREGON

Temporary Child Care and Crisis Nurseries in Oregon
Department of Health and Social Services
P.O. Box 231
Portland, OR 97207
(503) 229-5806

Description: New program providing temporary non-medical care for handicapped children, children with chronic or terminal illnesses, and abused or neglected children; designed to alleviate social, emotional and financial stress among their families
$ Given: Undetermined
Contact: Kristine Gebbie

PENNSYLVANIA

Temporary Child Care and Crisis Nurseries in Pennsylvania
Department of Health and Social Services
P.O. Box 90
Harrisburg, PA 17108
(717) 787-6436

Description: New program providing temporary non-medical care for handicapped children, children with chronic or terminal illnesses, and abused or neglected children; designed to alleviate social, emotional and financial stress among their families
$ Given: Undetermined
Contact: N. Mark Richards

RHODE ISLAND

Temporary Child Care and Crisis Nurseries in Rhode Island
Department of Health and Social Services
75 Davis Street
Providence, RI 02908
(401) 277-2231

Description: New program providing temporary non-medical care for handicapped children, children with chronic or terminal illnesses, and abused or neglected children; designed to alleviate social, emotional and financial stress among their families
$ Given: Undetermined
Contact: H. Denman Scott

SOUTH CAROLINA

Temporary Child Care and Crisis Nurseries in South Carolina
Department of Health and Social Services
2600 Bull Street
Columbia, SC 29201
(803) 734-4880

Description: New program providing temporary non-medical care for handicapped children, children with chronic or terminal illnesses, and abused or neglected children; designed to alleviate social, emotional and financial stress among their families
$ Given: Undetermined
Contact: Michael D. Jarrett

SOUTH DAKOTA

Temporary Child Care and Crisis Nurseries in South Dakota
Department of Health and Social Services
523 East Capitol Avenue
Pierre, SD 57501
(605) 773-3361

Description: New program providing temporary non-medical care for handicapped children, children with chronic or terminal illnesses, and abused or neglected children; designed to alleviate social, emotional and financial stress among their families
$ Given: Undetermined
Contact: Katherine Kinsman

TENNESSEE

Temporary Child Care and Crisis Nurseries in Tennessee
Department of Health and Social Services
436 6th Avenue, North, Room 100
Nashville, TN 37219
(615) 741-3111

Description: New program providing temporary non-medical care for handicapped children, children with chronic or terminal illnesses, and abused or neglected children; designed to alleviate social, emotional and financial stress among their families
$ Given: Undetermined
Contact: J.W. Luna

SPECIAL POPULATION FUNDING

. . . .

TEXAS

Temporary Child Care and Crisis Nurseries in Texas
Department of Health and Social Services
1100 West 49th Street
Austin, TX 78756
(512) 458-7375

Description: New program providing temporary non-medical care for handicapped children, children with chronic or terminal illnesses, and abused or neglected children; designed to alleviate social, emotional and financial stress among their families
$ Given: Undetermined
Contact: Robert Bernstein

UTAH

Temporary Child Care and Crisis Nurseries in Utah
Department of Health and Social Services
288 North 1460 West
Salt Lake City, UT 84116
(801) 538-6930

Description: New program providing temporary non-medical care for handicapped children, children with chronic or terminal illnesses, and abused or neglected children; designed to alleviate social, emotional and financial stress among their families
$ Given: Undetermined
Contact: Suzanne Dandoy

VERMONT

Temporary Child Care and Crisis Nurseries in Vermont
Department of Health and Social Services
60 Main Street
Burlington, VT 05402
(802) 863-7280

Description: New program providing temporary non-medical care for handicapped children, children with chronic or terminal illnesses, and abused or neglected children; designed to alleviate social, emotional and financial stress among their families
$ Given: Undetermined
Contact: Roberta Coffin

VIRGINIA

Temporary Child Care and Crisis Nurseries in Virginia
Department of Health and Social Services
109 Governor Street
Richmond, VA 23219
(804) 786-3561

Description: New program providing temporary non-medical care for handicapped children, children with chronic or terminal illnesses, and abused or neglected children; designed to alleviate social, emotional and financial stress among their families
$ Given: Undetermined
Contact: M.G. Buttery

WASHINGTON

Temporary Child Care and Crisis Nurseries in Washington
Department of Health and Social Services
Mail Stop ET 11,
P.O. Box 9709
Olympia, WA 98504
(206) 753-5936

Description: New program providing temporary non-medical care for handicapped children, children with chronic or terminal illnesses, and abused or neglected children; designed to alleviate social, emotional and financial stress among their families
$ Given: Undetermined
Contact: Robert Rolfs

WEST VIRGINIA

Temporary Child Care and Crisis Nurseries in West Virginia
Department of Health and Social Services
State Office Building 3,
Room 206
Charleston, WV 25305
(304) 348-2971

Description: New program providing temporary non-medical care for handicapped children, children with chronic or terminal illnesses, and abused or neglected children; designed to alleviate social, emotional and financial stress among their families
$ Given: Undetermined
Contact: David Heydinger

SPECIAL POPULATION FUNDING

. . . .

WISCONSIN

**Temporary Child Care
and Crisis Nurseries in
Wisconsin**
Department of Health and
Social Services
One West Wilson Street
Madison, WI 53701
(608) 266-1511

Description: New program providing temporary non-medical care for handicapped children, children with chronic or terminal illnesses, and abused or neglected children; designed to alleviate social, emotional and financial stress among their families
$ Given: Undetermined
Contact: George F. MacKenzie

WYOMING

**Temporary Child Care
and Crisis Nurseries in
Wyoming**
Department of Health and
Social Services
2300 Capitol Avenue
Cheyenne, WY 82002
(307) 777-6464

Description: New program providing temporary non-medical care for handicapped children, children with chronic or terminal illnesses, and abused or neglected children; designed to alleviate social, emotional and financial stress among their families
$ Given: Undetermined
Contact: Larry Meuli

SERVICES FOR DISABLED CHILDREN
(*Only parents of children up to 6 years old may apply*)

ALABAMA

Handicapped Infants and Toddlers Early Intervention Grants for Alabama
Department of Health and Social Services
434 Monroe Street, Room 381
Montgomery, AL 36130
(205) 261-5052

Description: New program providing comprehensive, coordinated multidisciplinary services — including appropriate day care — for handicapped infants and toddlers
$ Given: Undetermined
Contact: Claude Fox

ALASKA

Handicapped Infants and Toddlers Early Intervention Grants for Alaska
Department Health and Social Services
350 Main Street
Juneau, AK 99822
(907) 465-3030

Description: New program providing comprehensive, coordinated multidisciplinary services — including appropriate day care — for handicapped infants and toddlers
$ Given: Undetermined
Contact: Myra Munsen

ARIZONA

Handicapped Infants and Toddlers Early Intervention Grants for Arizona
Department of Health and Social Services
1740 West Adams Street
Phoenix, AZ 85007
(602) 542-1024

Description: New program providing comprehensive, coordinated multidisciplinary services — including appropriate day care — for handicapped infants and toddlers
$ Given: Undetermined
Contact: Ted Williams

. . . .

CALIFORNIA

Handicapped Infants and Toddlers Early Intervention Grants for California
Department of Health and Social Services
714 P Street, Room 1253
Sacramento, CA 95814
(916) 445-1248

Description: New program providing comprehensive, coordinated multidisciplinary services — including appropriate day care — for handicapped infants and toddlers
$ Given: Undetermined
Contact: Kenneth Kizer

COLORADO

Handicapped Infants and Toddlers Early Intervention Grants for Colorado
Department of Health and Social Services
4210 East 11th
Denver, CO 80220
(303) 331-4510

Description: New program providing comprehensive, coordinated multidisciplinary services — including appropriate day care — for handicapped infants and toddlers
$ Given: Undetermined
Contact: Thomas Vernon

CONNECTICUT

Handicapped Infants and Toddlers Early Intervention Grants for Connecticut
Department of Health and Social Services
150 Washington Street
Hartford, CT 06106
(203) 566-2038

Description: New program providing comprehensive, coordinated multidisciplinary services — including appropriate day care — for handicapped infants and toddlers
$ Given: Undetermined
Contact: Fredrick Adams

DELAWARE

Handicapped Infants and Toddlers Early Intervention Grants for Delaware
Department of Health and Social Services
P.O. Box 637
Dover, DE 19903
(302) 736-4701

Description: New program providing comprehensive, coordinated multidisciplinary services — including appropriate day care — for handicapped infants and toddlers
$ Given: Undetermined
Contact: Lyman Olsen

FLORIDA

Handicapped Infants and Toddlers Early Intervention Grants for Florida
Department of Health and Social Services
1323 Winewood Road, Room 115
Tallahassee, FL 32399
(904) 487-2705

Description: New program providing comprehensive, coordinated multidisciplinary services — including appropriate day care — for handicapped infants and toddlers
$ Given: Undetermined
Contact: Charles Mahan

GEORGIA

Handicapped Infants and Toddlers Early Intervention Grants for Georgia
Department of Health and Social Services
878 Peachtree Street, NE, Suite 201
Atlanta, GA 30309
(404) 894-7505

Description: New program providing comprehensive, coordinated multidisciplinary services — including appropriate day care — for handicapped infants and toddlers
$ Given: Undetermined
Contact: James Alley

SPECIAL POPULATION FUNDING

. . . .

HAWAII

Handicapped Infants and Toddlers Early Intervention Grants for Hawaii
Department of Health and Social Services
P.O. Box 3378
Honolulu, HI 96801
(808) 548-6505

Description: New program providing comprehensive, coordinated multidisciplinary services — including appropriate day care — for handicapped infants and toddlers
$ Given: Undetermined
Contact: John C. Lewin

IDAHO

Handicapped Infants and Toddlers Early Intervention Grants for Idaho
Department of Health and Social Services
450 West State Street,
4th Floor
Boise, ID 83720
(208) 334-5930

Description: New program providing comprehensive, coordinated multidisciplinary services — including appropriate day care — for handicapped infants and toddlers
$ Given: Undetermined
Contact: Fritz DixonLewin

ILLINOIS

Handicapped Infants and Toddlers Early Intervention Grants for Illinois
Department of Health and Social Services
535 West Jefferson Street
Springfield, IL 62761
(217) 782-4977

Description: New program providing comprehensive, coordinated multidisciplinary services — including appropriate day care — for handicapped infants and toddlers
$ Given: Undetermined
Contact: Bernard Turnock

INDIANA

Handicapped Infants and Toddlers Early Intervention Grants for Indiana
Department of Health and Social Services
1330 West Michigan Street
Indianapolis, IN 46206
(317) 633-8400

Description: New program providing comprehensive, coordinated multidisciplinary services — including appropriate day care — for handicapped infants and toddlers
$ Given: Undetermined
Contact: Woodrow Myers

IOWA

Handicapped Infants and Toddlers Early Intervention Grants for Iowa
Department of Health and Social Services
East 12th & Walnut Streets
Des Moines, IA 50319
(515) 281-5605

Description: New program providing comprehensive, coordinated multidisciplinary services — including appropriate day care — for handicapped infants and toddlers
$ Given: Undetermined
Contact: Mary Ellis

KANSAS

Handicapped Infants and Toddlers Early Intervention Grants for Kansas
Department of Health and Social Services
900 SW Jackson
Topeka, KS 66612
(913) 296-1343

Description: New program providing comprehensive, coordinated multidisciplinary services — including appropriate day care — for handicapped infants and toddlers
$ Given: Undetermined
Contact: Charles Konigsberg

SPECIAL POPULATION FUNDING

KENTUCKY

Handicapped Infants and Toddlers Early Intervention Grants for Kentucky
Department of Health and Social Services
275 East Main Street, First Floor
Frankfort, KY 40601
(502) 564-4770

Description: New program providing comprehensive, coordinated multidisciplinary services — including appropriate day care — for handicapped infants and toddlers
$ Given: Undetermined
Contact: Carlos Hernandez

LOUISIANA

Handicapped Infants and Toddlers Early Intervention Grants for Louisiana
Department of Health and Social Services
P.O. Box 60630
Baton Rouge, LA 70160
(504) 568-5051

Description: New program providing comprehensive, coordinated multidisciplinary services — including appropriate day care — for handicapped infants and toddlers
$ Given: Undetermined
Contact: Carlos Carbo

MAINE

Handicapped Infants and Toddlers Early Intervention Grants for Maine
Department of Health and Social Services
151 Capitol Street
Augusta, ME 04333
(207) 289-3201

Description: New program providing comprehensive, coordinated multidisciplinary services — including appropriate day care — for handicapped infants and toddlers
$ Given: Undetermined
Contact: Helen Zidowecki

MARYLAND

Handicapped Infants and Toddlers Early Intervention Grants for Maryland
Department of Health and Social Services
201 Preston Street
Baltimore, MD 21201
(301) 225-6500

Description: New program providing comprehensive, coordinated multidisciplinary services — including appropriate day care — for handicapped infants and toddlers
$ Given: Undetermined
Contact: Adele Wilzack

MASSACHUSETTS

Handicapped Infants and Toddlers Early Intervention Grants for Massachusetts
Department of Health and Social Services
150 Tremont Street
Boston, MA 02111
(617) 727-0201

Description: New program providing comprehensive, coordinated multidisciplinary services — including appropriate day care — for handicapped infants and toddlers
$ Given: Undetermined
Contact: Deborah Prothrow-Stith

MICHIGAN

Handicapped Infants and Toddlers Early Intervention Grants for Michigan
Department of Health and Social Services
P.O. Box 30195
Lansing, MI 48909
(517) 335-8024

Description: New program providing comprehensive, coordinated multidisciplinary services — including appropriate day care — for handicapped infants and toddlers
$ Given: Undetermined
Contact: Raj Weiner

SPECIAL POPULATION FUNDING

. . . .

MINNESOTA

Handicapped Infants and Toddlers Early Intervention Grants for Minnesota
Department of Health and Social Services
717 Delaware Street, SE, Room 262
Minneapolis, MN 55440
(612) 623-5460

Description: New program providing comprehensive, coordinated multidisciplinary services — including appropriate day care — for handicapped infants and toddlers
$ Given: Undetermined
Contact: Mary Ashton

MISSISSIPPI

Handicapped Infants and Toddlers Early Intervention Grants for Mississippi
Department of Health and Social Services
2423 North State Street
Jackson, MS 39215
(601) 960-7634

Description: New program providing comprehensive, coordinated multidisciplinary services — including appropriate day care — for handicapped infants and toddlers
$ Given: Undetermined
Contact: Alton Cobb

MISSOURI

Handicapped Infants and Toddlers Early Intervention Grants for Missouri
Department of Health and Social Services
P.O. Box 570
Jefferson City, MO 65102
(314) 751-6002

Description: New program providing comprehensive, coordinated multidisciplinary services — including appropriate day care — for handicapped infants and toddlers
$ Given: Undetermined
Contact: Robert Harmon

MONTANA

Handicapped Infants and Toddlers Early Intervention Grants for Montana
Department of Health and Social Services
Cogswell Building, Room C108
Helena, MT 59620
(406) 444-2544

Description: New program providing comprehensive, coordinated multidisciplinary services — including appropriate day care — for handicapped infants and toddlers
$ Given: Undetermined
Contact: John Drynan

NEBRASKA

Handicapped Infants and Toddlers Early Intervention Grants for Nebraska
Department of Health and Social Services
301 Centennial Mall, South
Lincoln, NE 68509
(402) 471-2133

Description: New program providing comprehensive, coordinated multidisciplinary services — including appropriate day care — for handicapped infants and toddlers
$ Given: Undetermined
Contact: Gregg Wright

NEVADA

Handicapped Infants and Toddlers Early Intervention Grants for Nevada
Department of Health and Social Services
505 East King Street
Carson City, NV 89710
(702) 885-4740

Description: New program providing comprehensive, coordinated multidisciplinary services — including appropriate day care — for handicapped infants and toddlers
$ Given: Undetermined
Contact: Joseph Q. Jarvis

SPECIAL POPULATION FUNDING

• •

NEW HAMPSHIRE

Handicapped Infants and Toddlers Early Intervention Grants for New Hampshire
Department of Health and Social Services
6 Hazen Drive
Concord, NH 03301
(603) 271-4501

Description: New program providing comprehensive, coordinated multidisciplinary services — including appropriate day care — for handicapped infants and toddlers
$ Given: Undetermined
Contact: William T. Wallace

NEW JERSEY

Handicapped Infants and Toddlers Early Intervention Grants for New Jersey
Department of Health and Social Services
CN 360
Trenton, NJ 08625
(609) 292-7837

Description: New program providing comprehensive, coordinated multidisciplinary services — including appropriate day care — for handicapped infants and toddlers
$ Given: Undetermined
Contact: Molly Joel Coye

NEW MEXICO

Handicapped Infants and Toddlers Early Intervention Grants for New Mexico
Department of Health and Social Services
1190 St. Francis Drive
Santa Fe, NM 87504
(505) 827-0020

Description: New program providing comprehensive, coordinated multidisciplinary services — including appropriate day care — for handicapped infants and toddlers
$ Given: Undetermined
Contact: Roy McKeag

NEW YORK

Handicapped Infants and Toddlers Early Intervention Grants for New York
Department of Health and Social Services
Corning Tower, Room 1408
Albany, NY 12237
(518) 474-2011

Description: New program providing comprehensive, coordinated multidisciplinary services — including appropriate day care — for handicapped infants and toddlers
$ Given: Undetermined
Contact: David Axelrod

NORTH CAROLINA

Handicapped Infants and Toddlers Early Intervention Grants for North Carolina
Department of Health and Social Services
225 North McDowell Street
Raleigh, NC 27602
(919) 733-3446

Description: New program providing comprehensive, coordinated multidisciplinary services — including appropriate day care — for handicapped infants and toddlers
$ Given: Undetermined
Contact: Ronald Levine

NORTH DAKOTA

Handicapped Infants and Toddlers Early Intervention Grants for North Dakota
Department of Health and Social Services
State Capitol
Bismarck, ND 58505
(701) 224-2372

Description: New program providing comprehensive, coordinated multidisciplinary services — including appropriate day care — for handicapped infants and toddlers
$ Given: Undetermined
Contact: Robert Wentz

SPECIAL POPULATION FUNDING

• •

OHIO

Handicapped Infants and Toddlers Early Intervention Grants for Ohio
Department of Health and Social Services
246 North High Street
Columbus, OH 43226
(614) 466-3543

Description: New program providing comprehensive, coordinated multidisciplinary services — including appropriate day care — for handicapped infants and toddlers
$ Given: Undetermined
Contact: Ronald Fletcher

OKLAHOMA

Handicapped Infants and Toddlers Early Intervention Grants for Oklahoma
Department of Health and Social Services
100 NE 10th Street
Oklahoma City, OK 73152
(405) 271-4200

Description: New program providing comprehensive, coordinated multidisciplinary services — including appropriate day care — for handicapped infants and toddlers
$ Given: Undetermined
Contact: Joan Leavitt

OREGON

Handicapped Infants and Toddlers Early Intervention Grants for Oregon
Department of Health and Social Services
P.O. Box 231
Portland, OR 97207
(503) 229-5806

Description: New program providing comprehensive, coordinated multidisciplinary services — including appropriate day care — for handicapped infants and toddlers
$ Given: Undetermined
Contact: Kristine Gebbie

• • • • • • • • • • • • • • • • • • •

PENNSYLVANIA

Handicapped Infants and Toddlers Early Intervention Grants for Pennsylvania
Department of Health and Social Services
P.O. Box 90
Harrisburg, PA 17108
(717) 787-6436

Description: New program providing comprehensive, coordinated multidisciplinary services — including appropriate day care — for handicapped infants and toddlers
$ Given: Undetermined
Contact: N. Mark Richards

RHODE ISLAND

Handicapped Infants and Toddlers Early Intervention Grants for Rhode Island
Department of Health and Social Services
75 Davis Street
Providence, RI 02908
(401) 277-2231

Description: New program providing comprehensive, coordinated multidisciplinary services — including appropriate day care — for handicapped infants and toddlers
$ Given: Undetermined
Contact: H. Denman Scott

SOUTH CAROLINA

Handicapped Infants and Toddlers Early Intervention Grants for South Carolina
Department of Health and Social Services
2600 Bull Street
Columbia, SC 29201
(803) 734-4880

Description: New program providing comprehensive, coordinated multidisciplinary services — including appropriate day care — for handicapped infants and toddlers
$ Given: Undetermined
Contact: Michael D. Jarrett

SPECIAL POPULATION FUNDING

. . . .

SOUTH DAKOTA

Handicapped Infants and Toddlers Early Intervention Grants for South Dakota
Department of Health and Social Services
523 East Capitol Avenue
Pierre, SD 57501
(605) 773-3361

Description: New program providing comprehensive, coordinated multidisciplinary services — including appropriate day care — for handicapped infants and toddlers
$ Given: Undetermined
Contact: Katherine Kinsman

TENNESSEE

Handicapped Infants and Toddlers Early Intervention Grants for Tennessee
Department of Health and Social Services
436 6th Avenue, North, Room 100
Nashville, TN 37219
(615) 741-3111

Description: New program providing comprehensive, coordinated multidisciplinary services — including appropriate day care — for handicapped infants and toddlers
$ Given: Undetermined
Contact: J.W. Luna

TEXAS

Handicapped Infants and Toddlers Early Intervention Grants for Texas
Department of Health and Social Services
1100 West 49th Street
Austin, TX 78756
(512) 458-7375

Description: New program providing comprehensive, coordinated multidisciplinary services — including appropriate day care — for handicapped infants and toddlers
$ Given: Undetermined
Contact: Robert Bernstein

• • • • • • • • • • • • • • • • • •

UTAH

Handicapped Infants and Toddlers Early Intervention Grants for Utah
Department of Health and Social Services
288 North 1460 West
Salt Lake City, UT 84116
(801) 538-6930

Description: New program providing comprehensive, coordinated multidisciplinary services — including appropriate day care — for handicapped infants and toddlers
$ Given: Undetermined
Contact: Suzanne Dandoy

VERMONT

Handicapped Infants and Toddlers Early Intervention Grants for Vermont
Department of Health and Social Services
60 Main Street
Burlington, VT 05402
(802) 863-7280

Description: New program providing comprehensive, coordinated multidisciplinary services — including appropriate day care — for handicapped infants and toddlers
$ Given: Undetermined
Contact: Roberta Coffin

VIRGINIA

Handicapped Infants and Toddlers Early Intervention Grants for Virginia
Department of Health and Social Services
109 Governor Street
Richmond, VA 23219
(804) 786-3561

Description: New program providing comprehensive, coordinated multidisciplinary services — including appropriate day care — for handicapped infants and toddlers
$ Given: Undetermined
Contact: M.G. Buttery

SPECIAL POPULATION FUNDING

WASHINGTON

Handicapped Infants and Toddlers Early Intervention Grants for Washington
Department of Health and Social Services
Mail Stop ET 11,
P.O. Box 9709
Olympia, WA 98504
(206) 753-5936

Description: New program providing comprehensive, coordinated multidisciplinary services — including appropriate day care — for handicapped infants and toddlers
$ Given: Undetermined
Contact: Robert Rolfs

WEST VIRGINIA

Handicapped Infants and Toddlers Early Intervention Grants for West Virginia
Department of Health and Social Services
State Office Building 3,
Room 206
Charleston, WV 25305
(304) 348-2971

Description: New program providing comprehensive, coordinated multidisciplinary services — including appropriate day care — for handicapped infants and toddlers
$ Given: Undetermined
Contact: David Heydinger

WISCONSIN

Handicapped Infants and Toddlers Early Intervention Grants for Wisconsin
Department of Health and Social Services
One West Wilson Street
Madison, WI 53701
(608) 266-1511

Description: New program providing comprehensive, coordinated multidisciplinary services — including appropriate day care — for handicapped infants and toddlers
$ Given: Undetermined
Contact: George F. MacKenzie

WYOMING

Handicapped Infants and Toddlers Early Intervention Grants for Wyoming
Department of Health and Social Services
2300 Capitol Avenue
Cheyenne, WY 82002
(307) 777-6464

Description: New program providing comprehensive, coordinated multidisciplinary services — including appropriate day care — for handicapped infants and toddlers
$ Given: Undetermined
Contact: Larry Meuli

Government Funding

The following chapter lists government agencies which can help you locate funding to assist with the high costs of day care for your children. Because the programs offered by government agencies vary widely and because many agencies offer new types of funding each year, the information here has been listed in a more generic form.

I suggest that, before you call the contact person in your state, you first make a list of every category in which you or your child may be fundable; i.e., are there demonstrated financial or other needs on the part of your family?, does your child require specialized care?, would locating a more affordable program be of assistance?, etc. In this fashion, you can cover every question leading to support and aid in one telephone call — by being able to describe precisely the kinds of funding you may be eligible for.

When you make the call, I suggest that you first ask, " What programs do you offer to assist parents/children with the costs of day care?" If they don't mention one that meets your particular need, ask more specific questions. If that agency doesn't offer such a program, many times they will be able to direct you to an agency that does. If they publish materials describing funding programs, request that they mail these to you, along with an application. Also make sure to find out if there is a deadline coming up, so that you will be able to return any applications by that time.

GOVERNMENT FUNDING

· · · · · · · · · · · · · · · · · · · ·

ALABAMA

Division of Family & Children's Services
Department of Human Resources
James E. Folsom Administrative Bldg.,
Room 503
64 N. Union Street
Montgomery, AL 36130–1801
(205) 261–3409

Contact: Paul Vincent, Director; Bob Hogue, Assistant Director; or Norma Manush, Assistant Director

ALASKA

Division of Family & Youth Services
Department of Health & Social
Services
Alaska Office Building, Room 404
350 Main Street
Juneau, AK

Mailing Address: Pouch H–05, Juneau, AK 99811
Contact: Yvonne M. Chase, Director, at (907) 465–3170; Martha A. Holmberg, Social Services Field Administrator, or Russ Webb, Social Services Field Administrator, both at (907) 465–3187

ARIZONA

Child Protective Services Section
Administration for Youth & Family
Division of Social Service
Dept. of Economic Security
4020 N. 20th Street, Suite 105
Phoenix, AZ 85016
(602) 266–0282

Contact: Marsha Porter, Program Supervisor

Division of Family Support
Department of Economic Security
1400 W. Washington Street
Phoenix, AZ
(602) 255–3596

Mailing Address: P.O. Box 6123, Phoenix, AZ 85005
Contact: Michael Q. Slattery, Assistant Director

• •

ARKANSAS

Division of Children & Family Services
Department of Human Services
7th & Main Streets
Little Rock, AR

Mailing Address: P.O. Box 1437, Little Rock, AR 72203–1437
Contact: Sharon Moone–Jochums, Deputy Director, or Pat Bailey-Page, Assistant Deputy Director of Field Operations, at (501) 682–8772; Richard Dietz, Assistant Deputy Director of Program Support, at (501) 682–8436; or Larry Meyer, Assistant Deputy Director of Administrative Services, at (501) 682–8731

CALIFORNIA

Family & Children Services Branch
Adult & Family Services Division
Department of Social Services
744 P Street, MS 9–101
Sacramento, CA 95814
(916) 445–7653

Contact: Albert A. Colon, Chief

Office of Child Abuse Prevention
Family & Children Services Branch
Adult & Family Services Division
Department of Social Services
744 P Street, MS 9–101
Sacramento, CA 95814
(916) 323–2888

Contact: Beth Hardesty Fife, Chief

COLORADO

Division of Child Welfare Services
Department of Social Services
State Social Services Building,
2nd Floor
1575 Sherman Street
Denver, CO 80203–1714
(303) 866–5957

Contact: Brian Golden, Acting Director

GOVERNMENT FUNDING

• •

CONNECTICUT

**Department of Children
& Youth Services**
170 Sigourney Street
Hartford, CT 06105

Contact: Amy B. Wheaton, Commissioner, or
Ralph E. Hughes, Deputy Commissioner, at
(203) 566–3536; or Janice M. Gruendel,
Deputy Commissioner, at (203) 566–3537

DELAWARE

Division of Child Protective Services
Department of Services for Children,
Youth, & Their Families
First State Executive Plaza
330 E. 30th Street
Wilmington, DE 19802
(302) 571–6410

Contact: Priscilla A. Brown, Acting Director

DISTRICT OF COUMBIA

Family Services Administration
Commission on Social Services
Department of Human Services
Randall School Building, Room 116
1st & I Streets, SW
Washington, DC 20024
(202) 727–5947

Contact: Dorothy J. Kennison, Administrator

FLORIDA

**Children, Youth & Families
Program Office**
Department of Health & Rehabilitative
Services, Building VIII
1317 Winewood Boulevard
Tallahassee, FL 32399
(904) 488–8763

Contact: Samuel M. Streit, Director; or Jean
Logan, Deputy Director

. . . .

GEORGIA

Assistance Payments Bursary
Division of Family & Children Services
Department of Human Resources
878 Peachtree Street, NE, Suite 406
Atlanta, GA 30309
(404) 894–5505

Contact: Alfra Dean Fisher, Director

HAWAII

Office of Children & Youth
Office of the Governor
Kapuaiwa Building, Room B10
426 Queen Street
Honolulu, HI
(808) 548–7582 or 548–7583

Mailing Address: P.O. Box 3044, Honolulu, HI 96802
Contact: Lynn N. Fallin, Director

IDAHO

Interstate Compact for Placement of Children
Family & Children's Services
Department of Health & Welfare
Towers Building, 450 W. State Street
Boise, ID 83720

Contact: V. Edward VanDusen, Administrator, at (208) 334–5688; Carolyn K. Ayres, Deputy Administrator, at (208) 334–5692; or Shirley Wheatley, Correspondent/Adoptions, at (208) 334–5697

ILLINOIS

Department of Children & Family Services
406 E. Monroe Street
Springfield, IL 62701
(217) 785–2509

Contact: Gordon Johnson, Director; or Michael Horstman, Executive Deputy Director

GOVERNMENT FUNDING

. . . .

INDIANA

Child Welfare/Social Services Division
Department of Public Welfare
141 S. Meridian Street, 6th Floor
Indianapolis, IN 46225

Contact: Susan J. Stanis, Director, at (317) 232–4420; or Cathleen Graham, Assistant Director, at (317) 232–4423

IOWA

Bureau of Adult, Children & Family Services
Division of Social Services
Department of Human Services
Hoover State Office Building, 5th Floor
1300 E. Walnut Street
De Moines, IA 50319–0114
(515) 281–5521

Contact: Ronald D. Stehl, Chief

KANSAS

Children in Need of Care
Youth Services
Department of Social & Rehabilitation Services
Smith–Wilson Building
300 S.W. Oakley
Topeka, KS 66606
(913) 296–3282

Contact: Jan Waide, Division Director

KENTUCKY

Division of Family Services
Department of Social Services
Human Resources Cabinet
Human Resources Bldg., 6th Floor West
275 E. Main Street
Frankfort, KY 40621
(502) 564–6852

Contact: Nancy L. Rawlings, Director

. . . .

LOUISIANA

**Division of Children, Youth
& Family Services**
Office of Community Services
Department of Social Services
1967 North Street
Baton Rouge, LA
(504) 342–2297

Mailing Address: P.O. Box 3318, Baton
Rouge, LA 70821
Contact: Marilyn Hayes, Director; or Robert
Hand, Deputy Director

MAINE

Division of Child & Family Services
Bureau of Social Services
Department of Human Services
Human Services Building
221 State Street
Augusta, ME
(207) 289–5060

Mailing Address: State House, Station 11,
Augusta, ME 04333
Contact: Barbara J. Churchill, Director

MARYLAND

Office for Children & Youth
Executive Department
State Office Building, Room 1502
301 W. Preston Street
Baltimore, MD 21201
(301) 225–4160

Contact: Dorothy V. Harris, Director

MASSACHUSETTS

Office for Children
10 West Street
Boston, MA 02111
(617) 727–8900

Contact: Mary Kay Leonard, Director; Joyce
Mathon–Trotman, Director, Advocacy; or
Marilyn Gallivan, Director, Licensing

GOVERNMENT FUNDING

. . . .

MICHIGAN

Office of Children & Youth Services
Department of Social Services
Commerce Center Building, 9th Floor
300 S. Capitol Avenue
Lansing MI
(517) 373–0093

Mailing Address: P.O. Box 30037, Lansing, MI 48909
Contact: L. Annette Abrams, Director

MINNESOTA

Division of Children Services
Department of Human Services
Human Services Building
444 LaFayette Road
St. Paul, MN 55155
(612) 296–5690

Contact: Janet Wiig, Director; or Charles Fecht, Assistant Director

MISSISSIPPI

Department of Public Welfare
515 E. Amite Street
Jackson, MS
(601) 354–0341

Mailing Address: P.O. Box 352, Jackson, MS 39205
Contact: Thomas H. Brittain, Jr., Commissioner; Carolyn Townes, Director, Bureau of Family & Children's Services; Max M. Cole, Bureau Director, Bureau of Economic Assistance; Al Soneson, Bureau Director, Bureau of Internal Affairs

MISSOURI

Division of Family Services
Department of Social Services
Broadway State Office Building
221 W. High Street
Jefferson City, MO

Mailing Address: P.O. Box 88, Jefferson City, MO 65103
Contact: Paula J. Willmarth, Director, at (314) 751–4247; Melody A. Emmert, Deputy Director, at (314) 751–2882; Gregory A. Vadner, Deputy Director, at (314) 751–3124; or David Vogel, Deputy Director, at (314) 751–4249

. . . .

MONTANA

Department of Family Services
48 N. Last Chance Gulch
Helena, MT

Mailing Address: P.O. Box 8005, Helena, MT
59601
Contact: Eugene Huntington, Director

NEBRASKA

Center for Children & Youth
Department of Social Services
Administration Building
2320 N. 57th Street
Lincoln, NE
(402) 471–3305

Mailing Address: P.O. Box 4585, Lincoln, NE
68504–0585
Contact: Kathleen Serghini, Director

NEVADA

Social Service Division
Department of Human Resources
2527 N. Canon Street
Carson City, NV
(702) 885–4766

Mailing Address: Capitol Complex, Carson
City, NV 89710
Contact: Thom Reilly, Chief

NEW HAMPSHIRE

**Bureau of Program Development &
Client Services**
Department of Health & Humna
Services
Health & Human Services Building
6 Hazen Drive
Concord, NH 03301
(603) 271–4456

Contact: Roger Dennison, Administrator

GOVERNMENT FUNDING

• •

NEW JERSEY

Division of Youth & Family Services
Department of Human Services
One South Montgomery Street
Trenton, NJ 08625

Contact: William Waldman, Director, or Marc Cherna, Assistant Director, at (609) 292–8716; Ted Joseph, Assistant Director, at (609) 292–1879; Bela Kanensky, Assistant Director, at (609) 292–9564; Jesse Moskowitz, Assistant Director, at (609) 292–8616; or Nicholas Sclera, Assistant Director, at (609) 292–4834

NEW MEXICO

Social Services Division
Human Services Department
PERA Building, Room 518
Santa Fe, NM
(505) 827–4372

Mailing Address: P.O. Box 2348, Santa Fe, NM 87504
Contact: Jack Callaghan, Director

NEW YORK

Family & Children's Services Operations Office
Division of Family & Children's Services
Department of Social Services
Ten Eyck Building, 9th Floor
40 N. Pearl Street
Albany, NY 12243
(518) 474–9607

Contact: Sanford Berman, Director

NORTH CAROLINA

Youth Advocacy & Involvement Office
Department of Administration
Elks Building, 1st Floor
121 W. Jones Street
Raleigh, NC 27603–1334
(919) 733–9296

Contact: Nancy J.R. Wells, Executive Director; or Pam A. Holland, Assistant Director

. . . .

NORTH DAKOTA

Children & Youth Family Services Division
Department of Human Serivces
State Capitol
Bismarck, ND 58505
(701) 224–4811

Contact: Donald L. Schmid, Director

Adoptions/Services to Pregnant Adolescent Single Parents
Children & Youth Family Services Division
Department of Human Serivces
State Capitol
Bismarck, ND 58505
(701) 224–4808

Contact: Virginia Petersen, Administrator

Child Protection Services
Children & Youth Family Services Division
Department of Human Services
State Capitol
Bismarck, ND 58505
(701) 224–4806

Contact: Gladys Cairns, Administrator

Early Childhood Services/Family-Based Services
Children & Youth Family Services Division
Department of Human Serivces
State Capitol
Bismarck, ND 58505
(701) 224–4809

Contact: Paul Ronningen, Administrator

. . . .

Foster Care Program
Children & Youth Family Services
Division
Department of Human Serivces
State Capitol
Bismarck, ND 58505
(701) 224–3587

Contact: Jean A. Doll, Administrator

OHIO

Department of Human Services
State Office Tower
30 E. Broad Street
Columbus, OH 43266–0423
(614) 466–1213

Contact: Daisy L. Alford, Deputy Director

Bureau of Compliance & Review
Division of Family & Children Services
Department of Human Services
State Office Tower
30 E. Broad Street
Columbus, OH 43266–0423
(614) 466–9824

Contact: Jean Schafer, Chief

OKLAHOMA

Child Welfare Services
Division of Children & Youth Services
Department of Human Services
Sequoyah Memorial Office Building,
Room 308
2400 N. Lincoln Boulevard
Oklahoma City, OK
(405) 521–3777

Mailing Address: P.O. Box 25352, Oklahoma
City, OK 73125
Contact: James Bohanon, Unit Supervisor; or
Martha Scales, Program Assistant Administrator

OREGON

Children's Services Division
Department of Human Resources
198 Commercial Street, SE
Salem, OR 97310
(503) 378–4374

Contact: Bill Thomas, Administrator; William
L. Carey, Acting Director, Client Services; or
Bobby Mink, Director, Support Services

PENNSYLVANIA

**Bureau of Child Welfare Planning &
Program Development**
Office of Children, Youth & Families
Department of Public Welfare
Health & Welfare Building, Room 131
Forster Street & Commonwealth Ave.
Harrisburg, PA

Mailing Address: P.O. Box 2675, Harrisburg,
PA 17105
Contact: Julia Danzy, Deputy Secretary, at
(717) 787–4756; or Lee Miller, Director, at
(717) 787–7756

RHODE ISLAND

**Department for Children & Their
Families**
Building 7
610 Mt. Pleasant Avenue
Providence, RI 02908
(401) 457–4650

Contact: James E. Patrick, Acting Director

Child Protective Services Division
Department for Children
& Their Families
Building 9
610 Mt. Pleasant Avenue
Providence, RI 02908
(401) 457–4950

Contact: Kenneth Fandetti, Assistant Director

GOVERNMENT FUNDING

. . . .

SOUTH CAROLINA

Office of Children, Family & Adult Services
Department of Social Services
North Tower Complex, Room 626
1535 Confederate Avenue, Extension
Columbia, SC

Mailing Address: P.O. Box 1520, Columbia, SC 29202–1520
Contact: Barry G. (Ms.) Dowd, Deputy Commissioner, at (803) 734–6182; or Ira Barbell, Executive Assistant, at (803) 734–5670

SOUTH DAKOTA

Child Protection Services
Division of Program Management
Department of Social Services
Richard F. Kneip Building
700 Governors Drive
Pierre, SD 57501
(605) 773–3227

Contact: Timothy R. Koehn, Program Administrator

TENNESSEE

Child Protective Services
Division of Social Services & Policy
Development
Office of Social Services
Department of Human Services
Citizens Plaza Building
400 Deadrick Street
Nashville, TN 37219
(615) 741–5939

Contact: Patricia B. Overton, Program Manager

Commission on Children & Youth
Department of Human Services
1510 Parkway Towers
404 James Robertson Parkway
Nashville, TN 37217
(615) 741–2633

Contact: Linda O'Neals, Executive Director

TEXAS

Services to Family & Children
Department of Human Services
John H. Winters Human Services
Building
701 W. 51st Street
Austin, TX
(512) 450–3020

Mailing Address: P.O. Box 2960, Austin, TX
78769
Contact: David C. Trejo, Deputy Commissioner; or Ron Thompson, Executive Administrator

UTAH

Division of Family Services
Department of Social Services
Social Services Building, 4th Floor
120 North, 200 West
Salt Lake City, UT
(801) 538–4100

Mailing Address: P.O. Box 45500, Salt Lake
City, UT 84115–0500
Contact: Jean Nielsen, Director; or William
Ward, Deputy Director

VERMONT

Division of Social Services
Department of Social & Rehabilitation
Services
Human Services Agency
Osgood Building
Waterbury Office Complex
103 S. Main Street
Waterbury, VT 05676
(802) 241–2131

Contact: Stephen R. Dale, Director

GOVERNMENT FUNDING

. . . .

VIRGINIA

Bureau of Child Welfare Services
Division of Service Programs
Department of Social Services
Nelson Building, Suite 244
1503 Santa Rosa Road
Richmond, VA
(804) 662–9695

Mailing Address: Blair Building, 8007
Discovery Drive, Richmond, VA 23229–8699
Contact: Sandra R. Whitaker, Chief

WASHINGTON

Division of Children & Family Services
Dept. of Social & Health Services
Mail Stop OB–41
Olympia, WA 98504
(206) 753–7002

Contact: Joyce Hopson, Director

WEST VIRGINIA

Bureau of Social Services
Families & Children Unit
Department of Human Services
State Office Building 6, Room B–850
1900 Washington Street, East
Charleston, WV 25305
(304) 348–7980

Contact: Pat Moore–Moss, Director

• •

WISCONSIN

Bureau for Children, Youth &
Families
Division of Community Services
Dept. of Health & Social Services
Wilson Street State Office Building,
Room 465
Madison, WI 53707
(608) 266–3036

Contact: Larry Reuter, Director

WYOMING

Bureau of Family Services
Division of Public Assistance & Social
Services
Dept. of Health & Social Services
Hathaway Building, Room 318
2300 Capitol Avenue
Cheyenne, WY 82002–0710
(307) 777–6285

Contact: Paul Blatt, Program Manager

AMERICAN SOMOA

Department of Human Resources
American Samoa Government
Pago Pago, AS 96799
011–684–633–4485

Contact: John Ah Sue, Director

Division of Social Services
Department of Human Resources
American Samoa Government
Pago Pago, AS 96799

Contact: Fualaau Hanipale, Program Director,
at 011-684-633-2696; or Cynthia Malala,
Administrative Assistant, at 011-684-633-4485

GOVERNMENT FUNDING

• •

GUAM

Child Welfare & Protective Services
Division of Social Services
Department of Public Health & Social Services
Agana, GU
011–671–477–8907 & 8928

Mailing Address: P.O. Box 2816, Agana, GU 96910
Contact: Marylou I. Taijernon, Supervisor

Social Services Administration
Division of Public Welfare
Department of Public Health & Social Services
California 1st Bank Building, Room 310
194 Herman Cortes Street
Agana, GU
011–671–477–8907 & 8928

Mailing Address: P.O. Box 2816, Agana, GU 96910
Contact: Edith V. Perez, Supervisor

Social Services Administration
Department of Public Health & Social Services
Agana, GU
011–671–472–6649

Mailing Address: P.O. Box 2816, Agana, GU 96910
Contact: Julita S.N. Lifoifoi, Human Services Administrator

PUERTO RICO

Department of Social Services
Old Naval Base, Isla Grande
Building 10, 2nd Floor
Santurce, PR
(809) 721–4624 or 722–7400

Mailing Address: P.O. Box 11398, Santurce, PR 00910
Contact: Carmen S. Zayas, Secretary

· ·

VIRGIN ISLANDS

Division of Children, Youth & Family
Department of Human Services
Barbel Plaza South
St. Thomas, VI 00802
(809) 774–4393

Contact: Judith Richardson, Administrator; or
Dilsa Rohan Capdeville, Assistant
Adminstrator

Corporate/ Employee Programs

. . . .

This chapter contains information about companies and corporations that provide several different kinds of child care related services. Many employees are aware of child care assistance only when an employer offers child care on-site, directly at the company's office or headquarters. Often, many employees are unaware of other forms of child care assistance their employers provide or could offer.

Companies listed in this chapter have been included on the basis of their total number of employees, with the largest in each area listed. Due to page restrictions, I have been unable to list all companies offering child care assistance. (Check with your employer to see if they provide any of the following services for your child care needs).

Generally, companies and corporations provide the following types of service for employee child care:

> **1. Child care centers either at (on-site) or near work (off-site)**. Some of these centers are free; others charge on a sliding scale. Some of the centers are run by the company. Others are run independently but exist primarily for the benefit of employees of one company or a group of companies.

> **2. Alternate day care programs provided by the employer**. These may include after-school care programs at school sites, summer camp programs, sick child care (to children at home or at an appropriate health facility), or day care

• •

for children provided through a family home
network organized by the employer and/or
employees at a particular work site (with the
blessing of the employer).

**3. Financial assistance and subsidies to
reduce the cost of child care**. Many companies offer subsidies to help offset the expensive
burden of child care. A subsidy may take the
form of a pretax set-aside (employees pay for
child care with funds deducted from salary *before*
taxes, making what they pay for child care non-
taxable income). Financial assistance from
employers may also take the form of direct
child care reimbursement, or may be part of an
individualized benefit package offered by
employers.

In many Northern European nations, day care is a
standard employer offering. At this writing I am sorry to
report that the record on US employer child care
assistance is rather dismal in comparison. Only 6,000 of
nearly six million employers provide some form of child
care assistance. Perhaps the example of the companies
listed in this chapter will motivate other companies to
do so. At the very least, this reference list can serve to
illustrate various child care services that employee
groups can encourage and lobby their employers (and
potential employers) to offer, citing "competitors" or
similar companies who are offering child care services to
employees.

Finally, for mothers returning to work, this list can point
out potential employers in their areas who are already
offering child care assistance.

ALABAMA

B.E. & K.
2000 International Park Dr.
Birmingham, AL 35243
(205) 969–3600

Type of Business: Construction
Type of Child Care: Mobile child care center at construction site
# of Employees: 2,900

Carraway Hospital
1600 N. 26th Street
Birmingham, AL 35234
(205) 226–2000

Type of Business: Hospital
Type of Child Care: Near or on-site center
# of Employees: n/a

Huntsville Hospital
101 Silven Road
Hunstville, AL 35801
(205) 533–8020

Type of Business: Hospital
Type of Child Care: Near or on-site center
# of Employees: 1,776

Southeast Alabama Medical Center
P.O. Drawer 6987
Dothan AL 36302
(205) 793–8111

Type of Business: Hospital
Type of Child Care: Financial aid
# of Employees: n/a

Springhill Hospital
3719 Dauphine Street
Mobile, AL 36608
(205) 344–9630

Type of Business: Hospital
Type of Child Care: Financial aid
# of Employees: n/a

CORPORATE/EMPLOYEE PROGRAMS

• • • • • • • • • • • • • • • • • • • •

ALASKA

Ketchian General Hospital
3100 Tongass Avenue
Ketchian, AK 99901
(907) 225–5171

Type of Business: Hospital
Type of Child Care: Near or on-site center
# of Employees: 418

Providence Hospital
3200 Providence Drive
Anchorage, AK 99508
(907) 562–2211

Type of Business: Hospital
Type of Child Care: Near or on-site center
# of Employees: 1,298

ARIZONA

America West Airlines
4000 E. Sky Harbor Blvd.
Phoenix, AZ 95034
(602) 894–0800

Type of Business: Airline
Type of Child Care: 24–hour near–site center
# of Employees: 11,869

Circle K Corp.
1601 N. 7th Street
Phoenix, AZ 85006
(602) 253–9600

Type of Business: Convenience market holding company
Type of Child Care: On or near-site center
# of Employees: 26,000

• • • • • • • • • • • • • • • • • •

Maricopa Medical Center
2601 E. Roosevelt
Phoenix, AZ 85008
(602) 267–5011

Type of Business: Hospital
Type of Child Care: Near-site center
# of Employees: 1,472

Phoenix Memorial Hospital
1201 S. Seventh Avenue
Phoenix, AZ 85036
(602) 258–5111

Type of Business: Hospital
Type of Child Care: Near or on-site center
# of Employees: 657

St. Joseph Hospital
350 W. Thomas Road
Phoenix, AZ 85013
(602) 285–3000

Type of Business: Hospital
Type of Child Care: Near or on-site center
# of Employees: 357

St. Joseph Hospital
350 N. Wilmot Road
Tucson, AZ 85710
(602) 296–3211

Type of Business: Hospital
Type of Child Care: Near or on-site center
# of Employees: 900

St. Mary's Hospital & Health Center
1601 W. St. Mary's Road
Tucson, AZ 85703
(602) 622–5833

Type of Business: Hospital
Type of Child Care: Near or on-site center
# of Employees: 1,184

CORPORATE/EMPLOYEE PROGRAMS

. . . .

ARKANSAS

Arkansas Children's Hospital
800 Marshall
Little Rock, AR 72202
(501) 370–1100

Type of Business: Hospital
Type of Child Care: Near or on-site center
# of Employees: 1,869

Baptist Medical Center
9601 Interstate 630
Little Rock, AR 72205
(501) 227–2000

Type of Business: Hospital
Type of Child Care: Near or on-site center
# of Employees: 2,386

St. Vincent's Infirmary
2 St. Vincent's Circle
Little Rock, AR 72205
(501) 660–3000

Type of Business: Hospital
Type of Child Care: Near or on-site center
# of Employees: 2,450

University of Arkansas Medical Sciences
4301 W. Markham
Little Rock, AR 72205
(501) 686–7000

Type of Business: Hospital
Type of Child Care: Near or on-site center
# of Employees: 1,444

• •

CALIFORNIA

American Savings & Loan
(Little Mavericks School of Learning)
701 E. Channel Street
Stockton, CA 95202

Type of Business: Commercial banking
Type of Child Care: On or near-site center
# of Employees: n/a

Apple Computer
20525 Mariani Avenue
Cupertino, CA 95014
(408) 996–1010

Type of Business: Personal computer manufacture
Type of Child Care: Near-site center; Pretax set-asides
# of Employees: 12,000

Atlantic Richfield Company
515 S. Flower Street
Los Angeles, CA 90071
(213) 486–3511

Type of Business: Oil production
Type of Child Care: Pretax set-asides
# of Employees: 20,507

Blue Cross
21555 Oxnard Street
Woodland Hills, CA 91367
(818) 703–2345

Type of Business: Health care
Type of Child Care: Near-site center
# of Employees: n/a

Centinela Hospital
555 E. Hardy Street
Inglewood, CA 90307
(213) 673–4660

Type of Business: Hospital
Type of Child Care: Near or on-site center
# of Employees: 1,528

CORPORATE/EMPLOYEE PROGRAMS

• • • • • • • • • • • • • • • • • •

Children's Hospital
4650 Sunset Boulevard
Los Angeles, CA 90027
(213) 660–2450

Type of Business: Hospital
Type of Child Care: Near or on-site center
# of Employees: 2,743

**Children's Hospital and
Health Center**
8001 Frost Street
San Diego, CA 92123
(619) 576–1700

Type of Business: Hospital
Type of Child Care: Near or on-site center
# of Employees: 1,338

**Commerce Clearing
House, Inc.**
Twin Oaks
One Thorndale Avenue
San Rafael, CA 94903

Type of Business: Publishing
Type of Child Care: Near-site center
# of Employees: n/a

Dataproducts Corp.
6219 DeSoto Avenue
Woodland Hills, CA 91365
(818) 887–8000

Type of Business: Computer printer manufacture and
repair
Type of Child Care: Near-site center
# of Employees: 3,500

Genetech, Inc.
460 Point San Bruno Blvd.
San Francisco, CA 94080
(41) 266–1000

Type of Business: Biotechnology
Type of Child Care: On–site center
# of Employees: 1,820

**Glendale Adventist
Hospital**
1509 Wilson Terrace
Glendale, CA 91206
(818) 409–8000

Type of Business: Hospital
Type of Child Care: Near or on-site center
# of Employees: 1,382

**Glendale Memorial
Hospital**
Central & Los Feliz
Glendale, CA 91225
(818) 502–1900

Type of Business: Hospital
Type of Child Care: Near or on-site center
# of Employees: 869

Great Pacific Ironworks
P.O. Box 150
259 Santa Clara Street
Ventura, CA 93002
(805) 643–6074

Type of Business: Sports apparel, backpacking equip-ment production
Type of Child Care: On-site center
# of Employees: n/a

G.T. Water Products, Inc.
5239 N. Commerce Avenue
Moorpark, CA 93021
(818) 529–2900

Type of Business: Drain-cleaning device manufacture
Type of Child Care: On–site school (K–high school)
# of Employees: 32 (very small company)

**Hemet Valley Medical
Center**
1117 Devonshire Street
Hemet, CA 92343
(714) 652–2811

Type of Business: Hospital
Type of Child Care: Near or on-site center
# of Employees: 1,076

CORPORATE/EMPLOYEE PROGRAMS

• • • • • • • • • • • • • • • • •

Hospital of the Good Samaritan
616 S. Witmer Street
Los Angeles, CA 90017
(213) 977–2121

Type of Business: Hospital
Type of Child Care: Near or on-site center
# of Employees: 1,444

KPFK Radio
2207 Shattuck
Berkeley, CA 94704
(415) 848–6767

Type of Business: Radio station
Type of Child Care: Financial aid
# of Employees: n/a

Levi Strauss & Co.
P.O. Box 7215
San Francisco, CA 94120
(415) 544–6000

Type of Business: Clothing manufacture
Type of Child Care: Financial aid
# of Employees: 31,000

Little Company of Mary Hospital
4101 Torrance Boulevard
Torrance, CA 90503
(213) 540–7676

Type of Business: Hospital
Type of Child Care: Near or on-site center
# of Employees: 1,053

Litton Industries
Computer Services
5490 Conaga Avenue
Woodland Hills, CA 91364
(818) 715–5200

Type of Business: Defense and high technology
Type of Child Care: Near-site center
# of Employees: 50,700

Loma Linda University Medical Center
P.O. Box 2000
Loma Linda, CA 92354
(714) 824-4302

Type of Business: Hospital
Type of Child Care: Near or on-site center
# of Employees: n/a

Long Beach Memorial Medical Center
2801 Atlantic Avenue
Long Beach, CA 90806
(213) 595-2311

Type of Business: Hospital
Type of Child Care: Near or on-site center
# of Employees: 3,313

Lost Arrow
259 W. Santa Clara Street
Ventura, CA 93001
(805) 643-8616

Type of Business: Outdoor clothing manufacture
Type of Child Care: Two on-site centers; Kindergarten; After-school care; Summer day camp; Pretax set-asides
# of Employees: 484

Mercy Hospital
2215 Truxtun
Bakersfield, CA 93301
(805) 327-3371

Type of Business: Hospital
Type of Child Care: Near or on-site center
# of Employees: 1,181

Methodist Hospital of Southern California
300 W. Huntington Drive
Arcadia, CA 91006

Type of Business: Hospital
Type of Child Care: Near or on-site center
# of Employees: 957

CORPORATE/EMPLOYEE PROGRAMS

• •

Morrison & Forester
345 California Street
San Francisco, CA 94104
(415) 677–7000

Type of Business: Law firm
Type of Child Care: Pretax set-asides
# of Employees: 1,524

O'Connor Hospital
2105 Forest Avenue
San Jose, CA 95128
(408) 947–2500

Type of Business: Hospital
Type of Child Care: Near or on-site center
# of Employees: 892

Oracle
500 Oracle Parkway
Redwood Shores, CA 94065
(415) 506–7000

Type of Business: Computer software production
Type of Child Care: On–site center; Pretax set–asides
# of Employees: 3,458

Paramount Studios
5555 Melrose Avenue
Los Angeles, CA 90038
(213) 468–5000

Type of Business: Entertainment
Type of Child Care: On–site center
# of Employees: 1,800

Pioneer Memorial Hospital
207 W. Legion Road
Brawley, CA 92227
(619) 344–2120

Type of Business: Hospital
Type of Child Care: Near or on-site center
# of Employees: 356

Prudential Insurance Co.
22935 Ventura Boulevard
Woodland Hills, CA 91364
(818) 712–9944

Type of Business: Insurance
Type of Child Care: Near-site center
# of Employees: n/a

**Redlands Community
Hospital**
350 Terracina
Redlands, CA 92373
(714) 793–3102

Type of Business: Hospital
Type of Child care: Near or on-site center
# of Employees: 769

Regis McKenna, Inc.
1755 Embarcadero Road
Palo Alto, CA 94303
(415) 494–2030

Type of Business: Marketing consultant
Type of child Care: Financial aid
# of Employees: 175

Rocketdyne
Division of Rockwell
International
6633 Canoga Avenue
Canoga Park, CA 91303
(818) 710–6300

Type of Business: Defense
Type of Child Care: Near-site center
# of Employees: n/a

St. Agnes Medical Center
1303 E. Herndon Avenue
Fresno, CA 93710
(209) 449–3000

Type of Business: Hospital
Type of Child Care: Near or on-site center
# of Employees: 1,904

CORPORATE/EMPLOYEE PROGRAMS

. . . .

St. Joseph's Medical Center
501 Buena Vista
Burbank, CA 91505
(818) 843–5111

Type of Business: Hospital
Type of Child care: Near or on-site center
# of Employees: 2,072

St. Lukes/Summit Health Care
2632 W. Washington Blvd.
Pasadena, CA 91109
(818) 797–1141

Type of Business: Hospital
Type of Child Care: Near or on-site center
# of Employees:\\394

San Diego Gas & Electric
101 Ash Street
San Diego, CA 92101
(619) 696–2000

Type of Business: Utilities
Type of Child Care: Near-site center
# of Employees: 4,800

San Diego Trust & Savings Bank
530 Broadway
San Diego, CA 92101
(619) 557–2508

Type of Business: Commercial banking
Type of Child Care: Near-site center
# of Employees: 1,400

Sharp Memorial Hospital
7901 Frost Street
San Diego, CA 92123
(619) 541–3400

Type of Business: Hospital
Type of Child Care: Near or on-site center
# of Employees: 2,433

Stuart Community Hospital
52nd and F Streets
Sacramento, CA 95819
(916) 454–3333

Type of Business: Hospital
Type of Child Care: Financial aid
# of Employees: 1,637

Syntex
3401 Hillview Avenue
Palo Alto, CA 94304
(415) 855–5050

Type of Business: Pharmaceutical manufacture
Type of Child Care: Near–site center
# of Employees: 5,554

Torrance Memorial Hospital
3330 Lomita
Torrance, CA 90505
(213) 325–9110

Type of Business: Hospital
Type of Child Care: Near or on-site center
# of Employees: 1,317

TRW Defense & Space Systems Group
1180 Kern Avenue
Sunnyvale, CA 94806

Type of Business: Defense
Type of Child Care: Financial aid
# of Employees: n/a

20th Century Insurance
20750 Ventura Boulevard
Woodland Hills, CA 91364
(818) 719–5300

Type of Business: Insurance
Type of Child Care: Near-site center
# of Employees: n/a

CORPORATE/EMPLOYEE PROGRAMS

. . . .

Verdugo Hills Hospital
1812 Verdugo Boulevard
Glendale, CA 91208
(818) 790-7100

Type of Business: Hospital
Type of Child Care: Near or on-site center
# of Employees: 468

**Veterans Administration
Medical Center**
5901 E. 7th Street
Long Beach, CA 90822
(213) 494-2611

Type of Business: Hospital
Type of Child Care: Near or on-site center
# of Employees: n/a

Wells Fargo & Co.
420 Montgomery Street
San Francisco, CA 94163

Type of Business: Commercial banking
Type of Child Care: Pretax set-asides; Child care costs
for overtime or travel reimbursed
# of Employees: 28,527

**White Memorial Medical
Center**
1720 Brooklyn Avenue
Los Angeles, CA 90033
(213) 268-5000

Type of Business: Hospital
Type of Child Care: Near or on-site center
# of Employees: 1,129

COLORADO

Boulder Community Hospital
N. Broadway at Balsam
Boulder, CO 80304
(303) 440–2273

Type of Business: Hospital
Type of Child Care: Near or on-site center
# of Employees: 1,151

Current, Inc.
1005 E. Woodwan Road
Colorado Springs, CO
80920
(719) 594–4100

Type of Business: Mail order house
Type of Child Care: Financial aid
# of Employees: 1,700

Penrose Community Hospital
P.O. Box 7021
Colorado Springs, CO
80917
(719) 591–3000

Type of Business: Hospital
Type of Child Care: Near or on-site center
# of Employees: n/a

Porter Memorial Hospital
2525 S. Downing Avenue
Denver, CO 80210
(303) 778–1955

Type of Business: Hospital
Type of Child Care: Near or on-site center
# of Employees: 1,592

Swedish Medical Center
501 E. Hampden
Englewood, CO 80110
(303) 788–5000

Type of Business: Hospital
Type of Child care: Near or on-site center
# of Employees: n/a

CORPORATE/EMPLOYEE PROGRAMS

• • • • • • • • • • • • • • • • • •

U.S. West
7800 East Orchard Road
Englewood, CO 80111
(303) 793–6500

Type of Business: Communications
Type of Child Care: Pretax set–asides
# of Employees: 64,623

CONNECTICUT

Aetna Life & Casualty
151 Farmington Avenue
Hartford, CT 06156
(203) 273–0619

Type of Business: Insurance
Type of Child Care: Near-site center
# of Employees: 45,000

American Can Co.
American Lane
Greenwich, CT 06830

Type of Child Care: Financial aid
# of Employees: n/a

Bind B. Associates
Route 5
P.O. Box 598
South Windsor, CT 06074

Type of Child Care: On or near-site center
# of Employees: n/a

• • • • • • • • • • • • • • • • • • •

Champion International
One Champion Plaza
Stamford, CT 06921
(203) 358–7000

Type of Business: Paper manufacture
Type of Child Care: On–site child care; Pretax set-asides
# of Employees: 21,265

CIGNA Co.
Kinder Care
Learning Centers Inc.
Hartford, CT 06152

Type of Business: Insurance
Type of Child Care: On or near-site center
# of Employees: n/a

**Connecticut Valley
Hospital**
Box 351
Middletown, CT 06457
(203) 344–2666

Type of Business: Hospital
Type of Child Care: Near or on-site center
# of Employees: 872

Greenwich Hospital
5 Perryridge Road
Greenwich, CT 06830
(203) 863–3000

Type of Business: Hospital
Type of child Care: Near or on-site center
# of Employees: 998

Hartford Hospital
80 Seymour Street
Hartford, CT 06115
(203) 524–3011

Type of Business: Hospital
Type of child care: Near or on-site center
# of Employees: 4,470

CORPORATE/EMPLOYEE PROGRAMS

. . . .

The Phoenix
One American Row
Hartford, CT 06115

Type of Business: Insurance
Type of Child Care: On–site center; Support for near–site center; Pretax set–asides
# of Employees: 2,004

Pitney Bowes
World Headquarters
One Elmcroft Road
Stamford, CT 06926
(203) 356–5000

Type of Business: Office equipment manufacture
Type of Child Care: Pretax set–asides
# of Employees: 22,784

St. Francis Hospital and Medical Center
114 Woodland Street
Hartford, CT 06105
(203) 548–4000

Type of Business: Hospital
Type of Child Care: Near or on-site center
# of Employees: 2,388

Southern New England Telecommunications
227 Church Street
New Haven, CT 06510
(203) 771–4662

Type of Business: Holding company
Type of Child Care: On or near-site center
# of Employees: 12,650

The Traveller
One Tower Square
Hartford, CT 06183

Type of Business: Insurance
Type of Child Care: Pretax set–asides; Child care costs for overtime reimbursed; Subsidies for child care
# of Employees: 34,652

Windham Hospital
112 Mansfield Avenue
Willimantic, CT 06226
(203) 423–9201

Type of Business: Hospital
Type of Child Care: Near or on-site center
# of Employees: 601

Xerox
P.O. Box 1600
Stamford, CT 06904
(203) 968–3000

Type of Business: Office machine manufacture
Type of Child Care: Pretax set–asides
# of Employees: 54,877

Yale University Medical Center
230 S. Frontage Road
New Haven, CT 06520
(203) 785–4242

Type of Business: Hospital
Type of Child Care: Near or on-site center
# of Employees: 4,097

DELAWARE

DuPont
1007 Market Street
Wilmington, DE 19898
(302) 774–1000

Type of Business: Chemical manufacture
Type of Child Care: Near–site centers; Sick care center
# of Employees: 104,000

CORPORATE/EMPLOYEE PROGRAMS

• • • • • • • • • • • • • • • • • • • •

DISTRICT OF COLUMBIA

Airline Traffic Publishing Company
P.O. Box 17415,
Dulles Airport
Washington, DC 20041
(703) 471–7510

Type of Business: Publishing
Type of Child Care: Financial aid
# of Employees: 385

The Bureau of National Affairs
1231 25th Street, NW
Washington, DC 20037
(202) 452–4200

Type of Business: Publishing
Type of Child Care: Pretax set–asides
# of Employees: 1,453

Capitol Hill Hospital
700 Constitution Avenue
Washington, DC 20002
(202) 269–8000

Type of Business: Hospital
Type of Child care: Near or on-site center
# of Employees: 750

Howard University Hospital
2041 Georgia Avenue, NW
Washington, DC 20060
(202) 865–6100

Type of Business: Hospital
Type of Child Care: Near or on-site center
# of Employees: 2,627

Marriott
One Marriott Drive
Washington, DC 20059
(301) 380–9000

Type of Business: Hotel/resort/food services management; Senior living services management
Type of Child Care: On–site center; Summer day camp; Pretax set–asides
# of Employees: 211,389

WJLA TV
4461 Connecticut Avenue
Washington, DC 20008
(202) 364–7777

Type of Business: Television station
Type of Child care: Near or on-site center
# of Employees: n/a

The World Bank
8100 H Street, NW
Washington, DC 20433

Type of Business: International banking
Type of Child Care: On or near-site center
# of Employees: n/a

WRC TV
4001 Nebraska Avenue
Washington, DC 20016
(202) 885–4000

Type of Business: Television station
Type of Child Care: Near or on-site center
# of Employees: n/a

WTTG TV
5151 Wisconsin Avenue
Washington, DC 20016
(202) 822–9363

Type of Business: Television station
Type of Child Care: Near or on-site center
# of Employees: n/a

WUSA TV
4001 Brandywine St., NW
Washington, DC 20016
(202) 364–3900

Type of Business: Television station
Type of Child Care: Near or on-site center
# of Employees: n/a

. . . .

FLORIDA

Alachua General Hospital
801 S.W. 2nd Avenue
Gainesville, FL 32601
(904) 372–4321

Type of Business: Hospital
Type of Child Care: Near or on-site center
# of Employees: 1,111

**American Bankers
Insurance Group**
11222 Quail Roost Drive
Miami, FL 33157
(305) 253–2244

Type of Business: Insurance
Type of Child Care: On-site care before/after school;
Pretax set-asides
# of Employees: 1,413

Baptist Hospital of Miami
8900 N. Kendall Drive
Miami, FL 33176
(305) 596–6503

Type of Business: Hospital
Type of Child Care: Near or on-site center
# of Employees: 2,107

Baptist Medical Center
800 Prudential Drive
Jacksonville, FL 32207
(904) 393–2000

Type of Business: Hospital
Type of Child Care: Financial aid
# of Employees: 1,932

Bay Medical Center
615 N. Bonita Avenue
Panama City, FL 32401
(904) 769–1511

Type of Business: Hospital
Type of Child Care: Near or on-site center
# of Employees: 1,002

• • • • • • • • • • • • • • • • • • • •

Cedars of Lebanon Hospital
1400 N.W. 12th Avenue
Miami, FL 33136
(305) 325–5511

Type of Business: Hospital
Type of Child Care: Near or on-site center
# of Employees: 1,642

Certified Grocers of Florida
P.O. Box 1510
Ocala, FL 32678
(904) 245–5151

Type of Business: Grocery, sundry, supplement supply
Type of Child Care: On or near-site center
# of Employees: n/a

Dalton & Lightfoot Development Corp.
The Rockinghorse Child
Care Centers of America
The Lakefront at Orlando
Central Park
Orlando, FL 32802

Type of Business: Development
Type of Child Care: Near-site center
# of Employees: n/a

Duda, A. & Sons, Inc.
Highway 426
Oviedo, FL 32765
(407) 365–2111

Type of Business: Farming and food processing
Type of Child Care: Near or on-site center
# of Employees: 1,600

Farm Bureau Insurance
5331 N.W. 34th Street
Gainesville, FL 32601

Type of Business: Insurance
Type of Child Care: On or near-site center
# of Employees: n/a

CORPORATE/EMPLOYEE PROGRAMS

• • • • • • • • • • • • • • • • • •

Good Samaritan Hospital
1300 N. Flagler Drive
West Palm Beach, FL 33407
(407) 848–5500

Type of Business: Hospital
Type of Child Care: Near or on-site center
# of Employees: 1,124

Grummon Aerospace Corp.
P.O. Box 1137
Stuart, FL 33495
(516) 575–0574

Type of Business: Aircraft engine & part production
Type of Child Care: Financial aid
# of Employees: n/a

Grummon Corp.
P.O. Box 3447
St. Augustine, FL 32085
(516) 575–0574

Type of Business: Aircraft research & development; Defense; Space vehicle equipment manufacture
Type of Child Care: Financial aid
# of Employees: n/a

Halifax Medical Center
P.O. Box 1990
Daytona Beach, FL 32015
(904) 254–4000

Type of Business: Hospital
Type of Child Care: Financial aid
# of Employees: n/a

Hialeah Hospital
651 E. 26th Street
Hialeah, FL 33013
(305) 693–6100

Type of Business: Hospital
Type of Child Care: Near or on-site center
# of Employees: 903

• • • • • • • • • • • • • • • • • • • •

Hollywood Memorial Hospital
3501 Johnson Street
Hollywood, FL 33021
(305) 987–2000

Type of Business: Hospital
Type of Child Care: Near or on-site center
# of Employees: 2,510

Holmes Regional Medical Center
1350 S. Hickory Street
Melbourne, FL 32901
(407) 727–7000

Type of Business: Hospital
Type of Child Care: Financial aid
# of Employees: 2,216

Holy Cross Hospital
4725 N. Federal Highway
Ft. Lauderdale, FL 33308
(305) 771–8000

Type of Business: Hospital
Type of Child Care: Near or on-site center
# of Employees: 1,580

Honeywell Avionics
13350 U.S. 19 South
Clearwater, FL 33545
(813) 531–4611

Type of Business: Defense
Type of Child Care: Financial aid
# of Employees: n/a

Lee Memorial Hospital
P.O. Drawer 2218
Ft. Myers, FL 33903
(813) 332–1111

Type of Business: Hospital
Type of Child care: Near or on-site center
# of Employees: 1,937

CORPORATE/EMPLOYEE PROGRAMS

. . . .

Memorial Hospital of Sarasota
1700 S. Tamiami Trail
Sarasota, FL 34239
(813) 955–1111

Type of Business: Hospital
Type of Child Care: Near or on-site center
# of Employees: 2,215

Mount Sinai Medical Center
4300 Alton Road
Miami Beach, FL 33140
(305) 674–1212

Type of Business: Hospital
Type of Child Care: Near or on-site center
# of Employees: 2,551

Munroe Regional Medical Center
P.O. Box 6000
Ocala, FL 32678
(904) 351–7200

Type of Business: Hospital
Type of Child Care: Financial aid
# of Employees: 1,036

Olin Corp.
P.O. Box 222
St. Marks, FL 32355

Type of Business: Chemical manufacture
Type of Child Care: Financial aid
# of Employees: n/a

Palmetto Hospital
2001 W. 68th Street
Hialeah, FL 33016
(305) 823–5000

Type of Business: Hospital
Type of Child Care: Financial aid
# of Employees: 1,036

• • • • • • • • • • • • • • • • • • •

Publix Super Markets
P.O. Box 407
Lakeland, FL 33807

Type of Business: Grocery sales
Type of Child Care: On or near-site center
# of Employees: n/a

St. Joseph's Hospital
3001 W. Buffalo Avenue
Tampa, FL 33607
(813) 870–4000

Type of Business: Hospital
Type of Child Care: Financial aid
# of Employees: 2,498

St. Vincent's Hospital
Box 2982
Jacksonville, FL 32203
(904) 387–7300

Type of Business: Hospital
Type of Child Care: Near or on-site center
# of Employees: 2,029

Tampa General Hospital
Davis Island
Tampa, FL 33601
(813) 251–7000

Type of Business: Hospital
Type of child Care: Financial aid
# of Employees: 3,602

Venice Hospital
540 The Rialto
Venice, FL 33595
(813) 485–7711

Type of Business: Hospital
Type of Child Care: Financial aid
# of Employees: 904

CORPORATE/EMPLOYEE PROGRAMS

• • • • • • • • • • • • • • • • • • •

Walt Disney World
P.O. Box 10,000
Lake Buena Vista, FL 32830

Type of Business: Entertainment park
Type of Child Care: On or near-site center
# of Employees: n/a

West Florida Hospital
8383 N. Davis Highway
Pensacola, FL 32523
(904) 478–4460

Type of Business: Hospital
Type of Child Care: Financial aid
# of Employees: 1,298

GEORGIA

**Atlanta Journal &
Constitution**
1400 Lake Hearn Drive, NE
Atlanta, GA 30319
(404) 843–5000

Type of Business: Newspaper, publishing, printing; Cable television services (Cox Enterprises)
Type of Child Care: Near-site center
# of Employees: n/a

Bowdon Manufacturing
127 N. Carroll
Bowdon, GA 30108
(404) 258–7242

Type of Business: Clothing manufacture
Type of Child Care: Near-site center
# of Employees: 115

• • • • • • • • • • • • • • • • • • • •

Cox Enterprises
1400 Lake Hearn Drive, NE
Atlanta, GA 30319
(404) 843–5000

Type of Business: Communications conglomerate
Type of Child care: Near-site center
# of Employees: 22,000

Dekalb Medical Center
460 Winn Way
Decatur, GA 30033
(404) 297–2700

Type of Business: Hospital
Type of Child Care: Near or on-site center
# of Employees: 1,834

Federal Reserve Bank
104 Marietta Street, NW
Atlanta, GA 30303
(404) 521–8500

Type of Business: Federal financial institution
Type of Child Care: Near-site center
# of Employees: n/a

First Atlanta Corp.
P.O. Box 4148
Atlanta, GA 30302
(404) 588–5000

Type of Business: Bank holding company
Type of Child Care: On or near-site center
# of Employees: 4,000

**Georgia Baptist
Medical Center**
285 Boulevard, NE
Atlanta, GA 30312
(404) 653–4000

Type of Business: Hospital
Type of Child Care: Near or on-site center
# of Employees: n/a

CORPORATE/EMPLOYEE PROGRAMS

. . . .

Georgia Pacific Corp.
133 Peachtree Street, NE
Atlanta, GA 30303
(404) 521–4000

Type of Business: Wood/wood by–products manufacture
Type of Child Care: Near-site center
# of Employees: 44,000

Grady Memorial Hospital
55 Coca Cola Place
Atlanta, GA 30335
(404) 589–4307

Type of Business: Hospital
Type of Child Care: Near or on-site center
# of Employees: 4,378

Hutcheson Medical Center
100 Gross Crescent Circle
Fort Ogelthorpe, GA 30742
(404) 858–2000

Type of Business: Hospital
Type of Child Care: Near or on-site center
# of Employees: 1,021

**Kennestone Regional
Health Care System**
677 Church Street
Marietta, GA 30060
(404) 426–2000

Type of Business: Hospital
Type of Child Care: Near or on-site center
# of Employees: 2,380

**Northeast Georgia
Medical Center**
743 Spring Street
Atlanta, GA 30501
(404) 535–3553

Type of Business: Hospital
Type of Child Care: Near or on-site center
# of Employees: 1,482

• • • • • • • • • • • • • • • • • •

Northside Hospital
100 Johnson Ferry Road
Atlanta, GA 30042
(404) 851–8000

Type of Business: Hospital
Type of child Care: Near or on-site center
# of Employees: 1,987

Piedmont Hospital
1968 Peachtree Road, NW
Atlanta, GA 30309
(404) 350–2222

Type of Business: Hospital
Type of Child Care: Near or on-site center
# of Employees: 2,246

Sherri Lynn, Inc.
P.O. Box 406
Zebulon, GA 30295

Type of Child Care: On or near-site center
# of Employees: n/a

South Fulton Hospital
1170 Cleveland
East Point, GA 30344
(404) 669–4000

Type of Business: Hospital
Type of Child Care: Near or on-site center
# of Employees: 1,161

University Hospital
1350 Walton Way
Augusta, GA 30910
(404) 722–9011

Type of Business: Hospital
Type of Child Care: Near or on site center
# of Employees: 2,942

• • • • • • • • • • • • • • • • • • • •

West Georgia
Medical Center
1514 Vernon Road
La Grange, GA 30241
(404) 882–1411

Type of Business: Hospital
Type of Child Care: Near or on-site center
# of Employees: 1,032

HAWAII

Maui Land &
Pineapple Co.
P.O. Box 187
Kahului, HI 96732
(808) 877–3351

Type of Business: Pineapple canning and land development
Type of Child Care: On or near-site center
# of Employees: 2,500

IDAHO

Kootenia Medical Center
2003 Lincoln Way
Coeur d'Alene, ID 83814
(208) 667–6441

Type of Business: Hospital
Type of Child Care: Near or on-site center
# of Employees: 667

. . . .

ILLINOIS

Allstate Insurance
Allstate Plaza North
Northbrook, IL 60062
(708) 402–5000

Type of Business: Insurance
Type of Child Care: Pretax set-asides
# of Employees: 55,138

Arthur Andersen & Co.
69 Washington Street
Chicago, IL 60602
(312) 580–0069

Type of Business: Accounting and management consulting
Type of Child Care: Pretax set-asides; Saturday on–site child care during tax season
# of Employees: 25,000

Leo Burnett
35 W. Wacker Drive
Chicago, IL 60601
(312) 220–5959

Type of Business: Advertising
Type of Child Care: Pretax set–asides; Sick child program
# of Employees: 2,180

Copley Memorial Hospital
502 S. Lincoln
Aurora, IL 60505
(708) 844–1030

Type of Business: Hospital
Type of Child Care: Financial aid
# of Employees: 684

Edgewater Hospital
5700 Ashland Avenue
Chicago, IL 60660
(312) 878–6000

Type of Business: Hospital
Type of Child Care: Near or on-site center
# of Employees: 7,116

• • • • • • • • • • • • • • • • • • • •

Fel–Pro
7450 N. McCormick Blvd.
Skokie, IL 60076
(708) 674–7700

Type of Business: Auto industry supply
Type of Child Care: On–site center; Emergency/sick child care; Summer camp
# of Employees: 1,941

Gottleib Memorial Hospital
701 W. North Avenue
Melrose Park, IL 60160
(708) 681–3200

Type of Business: Hospital
Type of Child Care: Near or on-site center
# of Employees: 859

Hewitt Associates
100 Half Day Road
Lincolnshire, IL 60069
(708) 295–5000

Type of Business: Corporate compensation and benefits program design
Type of Child Care: Pretax set–asides; Emergency/sick child care; Mothers' room for women who nurse; Child care costs reimbursed for after-hours work or travel
# of Employees: 2,688

Hines Veterans Administration Hospital
Fifth Avenue &
Roosevelt Road
Hines, IL 60141
(708) 343–7200

Type of Business: Hospital
Type of Child care: Near or on-site center
# of Employees: 2,695

Illinois Masonic Medical Center
836 W. Wellington
Chicago, IL 60657
(312) 975–1600

Type of Business: Hospital
Type of Child Care: Near or on-site center
# of Employees: 2,568

Lutheran General Hospital
1775 W. Dempster
Park Ridge, IL 60068
(708) 696–2210

Type of Business: Hospital
Type of Child Care: Near or on-site center
# of Employees: 3,157

**Memorial Hospital of
Carbondale**
404 W. Main Street
Carbondale, IL 62901
(618) 549–0721

Type of Business: Hospital
Type of Child Care: Financial aid
# of Employees: 548

Michael Reese Hospital
Lake Shore Drive
at 31st Street
Chicago, IL 60616
(312) 791–3545

Type of Business: Hospital
Type of Child Care: Near or on-site center
# of Employees: 3,556

**Northwest Community
Hospital**
5618 W. Eddy
Chicago, IL 60634
(312) 908–2000

Type of Business: Hospital
Type of Child Care: Near or on-site center
# of Employees: 3,796

Official Airline Guides
2000 Clearwater Drive
Oak Brook, IL 60521
(708) 574–6000

Type of Business: Publishing airline schedules and fares
Type of Child Care: On–site center; Pretax set–asides
# of Employees: 796

CORPORATE/EMPLOYEE PROGRAMS

• • • • • • • • • • • • • • • • • • • •

**Proctor Community
Hospital**
5409 Knoxville
Peoria, IL 61614
(309) 691–1000

Type of Business: Hospital
Type of Child Care: Near or on-site center
# of Employees: 816

Resurrection Hospital
7435 W. Talcott
Chicago, IL 60631
(312) 774–8000

Type of Business: Hospital
Type of Child Care: Near or on-site center
# of Employees: 1,975

**Rush–Presbyterian
St. Lukes Medical Center**
700 S. Paulina
Chicago, IL 60612
(312) 942–7000

Type of Business: Hospital
Type of child Care: Near or on-site center
# of Employees: 7,737

St. John's Hospital
800 E. Carpenter Street
Springfield, IL 62769
(217) 544–6464

Type of Business: Hospital
Type of Child Care: Near or on-site center
# of Employees: 2,703

St. Theresa Hospital
2615 Washington Street
Waukegan, IL 60085
(708) 249–3900

Type of Business: Hospital
Type of Child Care: Near or on-site center
# of Employees: 991

• • • • • • • • • • • • • • • • • • •

South Shore Bank
7054 S. Jeffery Boulevard
Chicago, IL 60649
(800) 669–7725

Type of Business: Commercial banking
Type of Child Care: Subsidized child care
# of Employees: 118

**Swedish Covenant
Hospital**
5145 N. California
Chicago, IL 60625
(312) 878–8200

Type of Business: Hospital
Type of child Care: Near or on-site center
# of Employees: 1,097

**Veterans Administration
Medical Center**
333 E. Huron Street
North Chicago, IL 60611
(312)943–6600

Type of Business: Hospital
Type of Child Care: Near or on-site center
# of Employees: 1,252

CORPORATE/EMPLOYEE PROGRAMS

• •

INDIANA

Lincoln National Corp.
1300 South Clinton Street
Fort Wayne, IN 46801
(219) 455–2000

Type of Business: Insurance
Type of child Care: Pretax set–asides
# of Employees: 11,690

Lutheran Hospital of Indiana
3024 Fairfield Avenue
Fort Wayne, IN 46807
(219) 458–2001

Type of Business: Hospital
Type of Child Care: Near or on-site center
# of Employees: 1,652

St. Francis Hospital
52 S. 16th Street
Beech Grove, IN 46107
(317) 787–3311

Type of Business: Hospital
Type of Child Care: Near or on-site center
# of Employees: 2,058

Salvation Army
1105 S. Waugh
P.O. Box 622
Kokomo, IN 45902

Type of Business: Provision to the needy
Type of Child Care: On or near-site center
# of Employees: n/a

Union Hospital
1606 N. Seventh Avenue
Terre Haute, IN 47804
(812) 238–7000

Type of Business: Hospital
Type of Child Care: Near or on-site center
# of Employees: 1,280

IOWA

Iowa Lutheran Hospital
University at Penn
Des Moines, IA 50316
(515) 263–5612

Type of Business: Hospital
Type of Child Care: Near or on-site center
# of Employees: 1,125

Iowa Methodist
Medical Center
1200 Pleasant Street
Des Moines, IA 50309
(515) 283–6212

Type of Business: Hospital
Type of Child Care: Near or on-site center
# of Employees: 2,808

Mercy Health Center
Mercy Drive
Dubuque, IA 52001
(319) 589–8000

Type of Business: Hospital
Type of Child Care: Near or on-site center
# of Employees: 1,125

Mercy Hospital
701 10th Street, SE
Cedar Rapids, IA 52403
(319) 398–6011

Type of Business: Hospital
Type of Child Care: Near or on-site center
# of Employees: 1.256

Mercy Hospital
Medical Center
1154 5th Avenue
Des Moines, IA 50314
(515) 247–3121

Type of Business: Hospital
Type of Child Care: Near or on-site center
# of Employees: 2,747

CORPORATE/EMPLOYEE PROGRAMS

. . . .

**Rockwell International/
Avionics Group**
400 Collins Road
Cedar Rapids, IA 52498
(319) 395–1000

Type of Business: Aviation
Type of Child Care: On or near-site center
# of Employees: n/a

**St. Luke's Regional
Medical Center**
2720 Stone Park
Sioux City, IA 51104
(712) 279–3500

Type of Business: Hospital
Type of Child Care: Near or on-site center
# of Employees: 1,200

KANSAS

Newman Hospital
12th & Chestnut
Emporia, KS 66801
(316) 346–6800

Type of Business: Hospital
Type of child care: Near or on-site center
# of Employees: 322

Riverside Hospital
2622 W. Central
Wichita, KS 67203
(316) 946–5000

Type of Business: Hospital
Type of Child Care: Near or on-site center
# of Employees: 324

St. Francis Regional Medical Center
929 N. St. Francis
Wichita, KS 67214
(316) 268–5000

Type of Business: Hospital
Type of Child Care: Near or on-site center
# of Employees: 2,802

Shawnee Mission Medical Center
9100 & 74th
Shawnee Mission, KS 66201
(913) 676–2000

Type of Business: Hospital
Type of Child Care: Near or on-site center
# of Employees: 1,539

University of Kansas Hospital
39th & Rainbow
Kansas City, KS 66103
(913) 588–5000

Type of Business: Hospital
Type of Child Care: Near or on-site center
# of Employees: 3,700

Veterans Administration Medical Center
Box 829
Topeka, KS 66601
(913) 272–3111

Type of Business: Hospital
Type of Child Care: Near or on-site center
# of Employees: 1,122

Wesley Hospital
550 N. Hillside Avenue
Wichita, KS 67214
(316) 688–2468

Type of Business: Hospital
Type of Child Care: Near or on-site center
# of Employees: 2,900

. . . .

KENTUCKY

**Community Methodist
Hospital**
1305 N. Elm Street
Henderson, KY 42420
(502) 827-7700

Type of Business: Hospital
Type of Child Care: Near or on-site center
# of Employees: 644

Jewish Hospital, Inc.
217 East Chestnut
Lousiville, KY 40202
(502) 587-4011

Type of Business: Hospital
Type of Child Care: Near-site center
# of Employees: 1,547

Norton Children's Hospital
Box 35070
Louisville, KY 40202
(502) 562-6000

Type of Business: Hospital
Type of Child Care: Near-site center
# of Employees: 1,804

**St. Elizabeth
Medical Center**
1 Medical Village Drive
Edgewood, KY 41017
(606) 344-2000

Type of Business: Hospital
Type of Child care: Near-site center
# of Employees: 2,235

St. Joseph Hospital
One St. Joseph Drive
Lexington, KY 40504
(606) 298-3436

Type of Business: Hospital
Type of Child Care: Near or on-site center
# of Employees: 1,430

St. Mary and Elizabeth Hospital
1850 Bluegrass Avenue
Louisville, KY 40215
(502) 361–6000

Type of Business: Hospital
Type of Child Care: Near or on-site center
# of Employees: 866

Western Baptist Hospital
2501 Kentucky Avenue
Paducah, KY 42001
(502) 575–2100

Type of Business: Hospital
Type of Child Care: Near or on-site center
# of Employees: 1,209

LOUISIANA

Baton Rouge General Medical Center
P.O. Box 2511
Baton Rouge, LA 70821
(504) 387–7000

Type of Business: Hospital
Type of Child Care: Near or on-site center
# of Employees: 1,378

Doctor's Hospital
1130 Louisiana Avenue
Shreveport, LA 71101
(318) 227–1211

Type of Business: Hospital
Type of Child Care: Near or on-site center
# of Employees: n/a

CORPORATE/EMPLOYEE PROGRAMS

• • • • • • • • • • • • • • • • • • • •

East Jefferson
General Hospital
4200 Houma Boulevard
Metairie, LA 70011
(504) 454–4000

Type of Business: Hospital
Type of Child Care: Financial aid
# of Employees: 1,772

Our Lady of Lourdes
Regional Medical Center
611 St. Landry Street
Lafayette, LA 70502
(318) 234–7381

Type of Business: Hospital
Type of Child Care: Near or on-site center
# of Employees: 985

Pendelton Memorial
Methodist Hospital
5620 Read Road
New Orleans, LA 70127
(504) 244–5474

Type of Business: Hospital
Type of Child Care: Near or on-site center
# of Employees: 808

Schumpert Medical
Center
915 Margaret Place
Shreveport, LA 71120
(318) 227–4500

Type of Business: Hospital
Type of Child Care: Near or on-site center; Financial aid
# of Employees: 2,228

Southern Baptist Hospital
2700 Napoleon Avenue
New Orleans, LA 70115
(504) 899–9311

Type of Business: Hospital
Type of Child Care: Near or on-site center
# of Employees: 1,556

Woman's Hospital
Box 95009
Baton Rouge, LA 70895
(504) 927–1300

Type of Business: Hospital
Type of Child Care: Near or on-site center
# of Employees: 752

MAINE

**Central Main
Medical Center**
300 Main Street
Lewiston, ME 04240
(207) 795–0111

Type of Business: Hospital
Type of Child Care: Near-site center
# of Employees: 855

UNUM
2211 Congress Street
Portland, ME 04122
(207) 770–2211

Type of Business: Insurance
Type of Child Care: On–site center; Pretax set–asides;
Low income child care subsidies
# of Employees: 4,324

CORPORATE/EMPLOYEE PROGRAMS

• • • • • • • • • • • • • • • • • • •

MARYLAND

Aspen Systems Corporation
1600 Research Boulevard
Rockville, MD 20850
(301) 251–5000

Type of Business: Data processing
Type of Child Care: Financial aid
# of Employees: 260

Baltimore Gas & Electric
Baltimore, MD 21201
(301) 234–5000

Type of Business: Utility
Type of Child Care: Near-site center
# of Employees: 9,100

Johns Hopkins Hospital
600 N. Wolfe Street
Baltimore, MD 21205
(301) 955–5000

Type of Business: Hospital
Type of Child Care: Near-site center
# of Employees: 5,506

MNB Financial
10 Light Street
Baltimore, MD 21202
(301) 244–5000

Type of Business: Banking and financial services
Type of Child Care: On–site center; Support for near-site centers; Pretax set-asides
# of Employees: 12,376

National Institutes of Health
9000 Rockville Pike
Bethesda, MD 20892

Type of Business: Health care, research
Type of Child Care: On or near-site center
# of Employees: n/a

Suburban Hospital
8600 Old Germantown Rd.
Bethesda, MD 20814
(301) 530–3100

Type of Business: Hospital
Type of Child Care: Near-site center
# of Employees: 1,226

MASSACHUSETTS

Berkshire Life Insurance
700 South Street
Pittsfield, MA 01201
(413) 499–4321

Type of Business: Insurance
Type of Child Care: On or near-site center
# of Employees: 286

Beverly Hospital
Herrick Street
Beverly, MA 01915
(508) 922–3000

Type of Business: Hospital
Type of Child Care: Near or on-site center
# of Employees: 993

Bolt, Beranck & Newman
10 Fawcett Street
Cambridge, MA 02238
(617) 873–2000

Type of Business: Computers, electronics, software production
Type of Child Care: Financial aid
# of Employees: 2,750

CORPORATE/EMPLOYEE PROGRAMS

• • • • • • • • • • • • • • • • • • • •

**Boston's Beth Israel
Hospital**
330 Brookline Avenue
Boston, MA 02215
(617) 735–2000

Type of Business: Hospital
Type of Child Care: Near-site center (soon to be on site)
# of Employees: 4,672

**Brigham & Women's
Hospital**
75 Francis Street
Boston, MA 02115

Type of Business: Hospital
Type of Child Care: Near or on-site center
# of Employees: 5,469

Children's Hospital
300 Longwood Avenue
Boston, MA 02115
(617) 735–6000

Type of Business: Hospital
Type of Child Care: Near or on-site center
# of Employees: 3,192

**Dana Farber
Cancer Institute**
44 Binney
Boston, MA 02115
(617) 732–3000

Type of Business: Hospital
Type of Child Care: Near or on-site center
# of Employees: 1,334

Chomerics
77 Dragon Court
Woburn, MA 01888
(617) 935–4850

Type of Business: Industrial manufacture
Type of Child Care: Financial aid
# of Employees: 780

Cushing Hospital
Box 9008
Framingham, MA 01701
(508) 872–4301

Type of Business: Hospital
Type of Child Care: Near or on-site center; Financial aid
# of Employees: 489

Digital Equipment
146 Main Street
Maynard, MA 01754
(508) 493–5111

Type of Business: Computer manufacture and maintenance
Type of Child Care: Pretax set–asides; Summer camp for children
# of Employees: 72,000

Flatley Company
5320 Hill Park
Braintree, MA 02184
(617) 848–2000

Type of Business: Hotel/motel construction; Television stations
Type of Child Care: Near or on-site center
# of Employees: 5,320

Grieco Bros. Inc.
Southwick
50 Island Street
Lawrence, MA 01840
(508) 686–3833

Type of Business: Clothing manufacture
Type of Child Care: On–site child care; Pretax set–asides
# of Employees: 650

GTE Laboratories
100 First Avenue
Waltham, MA 02254
(617) 890–9200

Type of Business: Communications systems
Type of Child Care: Near-site center
# of Employees: 9,000

CORPORATE/EMPLOYEE PROGRAMS

• • • • • • • • • • • • • • • • • • •

John Hancock
Financial Services
John Hancock Place
P.O. Box 111
Boston, MA 02117
(617) 572–6000

Type of Business: Insurance
Type of Child Care: On–site center; Pretax set–asides;
Child care cost reimbursement for overtime or travel
# of Employees: 5,200

Hill, Holliday, Connors,
Cosmopulos
200 Clarendon Street
Boston, MA 02116
(617) 437–1600

Type of Business: Advertising
Type of Child Care: Near–site center; Pretax set–asides
# of Employees: 387

Lowell General Hospital
391 Varnum Avenue
Lowell, MA 01854

Type of Business: Hospital
Type of Child Care: Near or on-site center
# of Employees: 840

Massachusetts Mutual
Life Insurance Co.
1295 State Street
Springfield, MA 01111
(413) 788–8411

Type of Business: Insurance
Type of Child Care: On or near-site center
# of Employees: 5,900

Mercy Hospital
Box 9012
Springfield, MA 01102
(413) 781–9100

Type of Business: Hospital
Type of Child Care: Near or on-site center
# of Employees: 1,448

• • • • • • • • • • • • • • • • • • • •

Middlesex County Hospital
775 Trapelo Road
Waltham, MA 02154
(617) 894–4600

Type of Business: Hospital
Type of Child Care: Near or on-site center
# of Employees: 321

**New England
Medical Center**
750 Washington
Boston, MA 02180
(617) 956–5000

Type of Business: Hospital
Type of Child Care: Near or on-site center
# of Employees: 2,659

**New England
Memorial Hospital**
5 Woodland Road
Stoneham, MA 02180
(617) 979–7000

Type of Business: Hospital
Type of Child Care: Near or on-site center
# of Employees: 844

Newton–Wellesley Hospital
2014 Washington
Newton, MA 02162
(617) 243–6000

Type of Business: Hospital
Type of Child Care: Near or on-site center
# of Employees: 1,629

Polaroid Corp.
750 Main Street
Cambridge, MA 01239
(617) 577–2000

Type of Business: Camera and accessories manufacture
Type of Child Care: Financial aid
# of Employees: 13,622

CORPORATE/EMPLOYEE PROGRAMS

• • • • • • • • • • • • • • • • • •

Polo Clothing Co.
15 Union Street
Lawrence, MA 01840
(508) 686–3841

Type of Business: Clothing manufacture
Type of Child Care: On or near-site center
# of Employees: 265

Stop & Shop
P.O. Box 369
Boston, MA 02101
(617) 770–8000

Type of Business: Supermarket & discount store operation
Type of Child Care: On or near-site center
# of Employees: 48,000

Stride Rite
5 Cambridge Center
Cambridge, MA 02142
(617) 491–8800

Type of Business: Children's shoe manufacture
Type of Child Care: On–site centers
# of Employees: 4,000

University of Massachu-setts Medical Center
55 Lake Avenue, North
Worcester, MA 01605
(508) 856–0111

Type of Business: Hospital
Type of Child Care: Near or on-site center
# of Employees: 3,133

Wang Laboratories
1 Industrial Avenue
Lowell, MA 01851
(508) 459–5000

Type of Business: Computer manufacture
Type of Child Care: On or near-site center
# of Employees: 21,300

MICHIGAN

Ann Arbor
Veterans Administration
Medical Center
2215 Fuller Road
Ann Arbor, MI 48105
(313) 769–7100

Type of Business: Hospital
Type of Child Care: Near or on-site center
# of Employees: 1,279

Blodgett Memorial
Medical Center
1840 Wealthy, SE
Grand Rapids, MI 49506
(616) 774–7444

Type of Business: Hospital
Type of Child Care: Near or on-site center
# of Employees: 1,345

Catherine McAuley
Health System
5301 E. Huron River Drive
Ann Arbor, MI 48106
(313) 572–3456

Type of Business: Hospital
Type of Child Care: On-site center; Pretax set–asides
# of Employees: 5,050

Dow Chemical
2020 Willard H. Dow Center
Midland, MI 48674
(517) 636–2253

Type of Business: Chemical manufacture
Type of Child Care: Before/after-school programs; Near-site centers; Sick child care; Summer program; Pretax set–asides
# of Employees: 30,364

Group 243
(part of Ross Roy Group)
1410 Woodridge Avenue
Ann Arbor, MI 48105
(313) 995–0243

Type of Business: Advertising
Type of Child Care: On–site center; Pretax set–asides
# of Employees: 96

CORPORATE/EMPLOYEE PROGRAMS

• • • • • • • • • • • • • • • • • • •

Henry Ford Hospital
2799 Grand Boulevard
Detroit, MI 48202
(313) 876–2600

Type of Business: Hospital
Type of Child Care: Near or on-site center
# of Employees: 8,646

Hurley Medical Center
1 Hurley Place
Flint, MI 48502
(313) 257–9237

Type of Business: Hospital
Type of Child Care: Near or on-site center
# of Employees: 2,429

Oakwood Hospital
18101 Oakwood Boulevard
Dearborn, MI 48124
(313) 593–7000

Type of Business: Hospital
Type of Child Care: Near or on-site center
# of Employees: 2,665

**St. Josephs Mercy
Hospital**
900 Woodward Avenue
Pontiac, MI 48053
(313) 858–3000

Type of Business: Hospital
Type of Child Care: Near or on-site center
# of Employees: 2,015

Steelcase
P.O. Box 1967
Grand Rapids, MI 49501
(616) 247–2710

Type of Business: Office furniture manufacture
Type of Child Care: Pretax set–asides
# of Employees: 13,800

· · · · · · · · · · · · · · · · · · · ·

MINNESOTA

Cardiac Pacemaker
4100 Hamline Avenue, North
St. Paul, MN 55112
(612) 638–4000

Type of Business: Cardiovascular product manufacture
Type of Child Care: On or near-site center
# of Employees: 1,100

Children's Hospital
345 N. Smith Avenue
St. Paul, MN 55102
(612) 298–8666

Type of Business: Hospital
Type of Child Care: Near or on-site center
# of Employees: 552

General Mills
P.O. Box 1113
Minneapolis, MN 55440
(612) 540–2311

Type of Business: Food production and restaurant operation
Type of Child Care: Discounts at child-care centers; Pretax set–asides
# of Employees: 84,000

Honeywell, Inc.
Honeywell Plaza
Minneapolis, MN 55408

Type of Business: Industrial automation, space and aviation
Type of Child Care: Financial assistance
# of Employees: 63,206

IDS Financial Services
(An American Express
Company)
700 IDS Tower
Minneapolis, MN 55402
(612) 372–3131

Type of Business: Financial planning, investment product sales
Type of Child Care: Pretax set–asides; Sick child subsidy; Child care costs reimbursed for overtime or travel
# of Employees: 3,600

. . . .

**3M (Minnesota Mining &
Manufacturing)**
3M Center
St. Paul, MN 55144
(612) 733–1110

Type of Business: Office supplies manufacture
Type of Child Care: Pretax set–asides; Subsidized in–home care for sick children
# of Employees: 49,000

Pillsbury Co.
200 S. 6th Street
Minneapolis, MN 55402
(612) 330–4966

Type of Business: Food production
Type of Child Care: Financial aid
# of Employees: 68,000

Wegmans
1500 Brooks Avenue
Rochester, MN 14692
(716) 328–2550

Type of Business: Supermarket chain
Type of Child Care: On–site center
# of Employees: 13,000

MISSISSIPPI

Jeff–Davis Memorial Hospital
Sergeant S. Prentiss Drive
Natchez, MS 39120
(601) 442–2871

Type of Business: Hospital
Type of Child Care: Near or on-site center; Financial aid
# of Employees: 456

Memorial Hospital of Gulfport
P.O. Box 1810
Gulfport, MS 39502
(601) 863–1441

Type of Business: Hospital
Type of Child Care: Near or on-site center
# of Employees: 119

St. Dominic–Jackson Memorial Hospital
969 Lakeland Drive
Jackson, MS 39216
(601) 982–0121

Type of Business: Hospital
Type of Child Care: Near or on-site center
# of Employees: 1,255

CORPORATE/EMPLOYEE PROGRAMS

• • • • • • • • • • • • • • • • • • • •

MISSOURI

Anheuser–Busch
1 Busch Place
St. Louis, MO 63118
(314) 577–2000

Type of Business: Brewery
Type of Child Care: Near-site center
# of Employees: 41,100

Baptist Medical Center
6601–A Rockhill
Kansas City, MO 64131
(816) 276–7000

Type of Business: Hospital
Type of Child Care: Near or on-site center; Financial aid
# of Employees: 982

**Cardinal Glennon
Children's Hospital**
1465 Grand Boulevard
St. Louis, MO 63104
(314) 577–5600

Type of Business: Hospital
Type of Child Care: Near or on-site center
# of Employees: 1,142

**Christian Hospital
Northeast/Northwest**
11133 Dunn Road
St. Louis, MO 63136
(314) 355–2300

Type of Business: Hospital
Type of Child Care: Near or on-site center
# of Employees: 2,530

Deaconess Hospital
6150 Oakland Avenue
St. Louis, MO 63139
(314) 768–3000

Type of Business: Hospital
Type of Child Care: Near or on-site center
# of Employees: 2,161

General Dynamics
Pierre LaClede Center
St. Louis, MO 63105
(314) 889–8200

Type of Business: Defense
Type of Child Care: On or near-site center
# of Employees: 102,000

Hallmark Cards
P.O. Box 419580
Kansas City, MO 64141
(816) 274–5111

Type of Business: Greeting card production
Type of Child Care: Pretax set-asides
# of Employees: 16,800

Indeeco
425 Hanley Industrial Court
St. Louis, MO 63144
(314) 644–4300

Type of Business: Electric heater and electronic control manufacture
Type of Child Care: On–site center
# of Employees: 317

Industrial Engineering & Equipment
288 Hanley Industrial Court
St. Louis, MO 63144–1508
(314) 644–4300

Type of Business: Production of central equipment, electronic units & devices
Type of Child Care: On or near-site center
# of Employees: n/a

McDonald Douglas
6038 Caroline Avenue
St. Louis, MO 63134
(314) 232–0232

Type of Business: Defense
Type of Child Care: On or near-site center
# of Employees: 127,926

CORPORATE/EMPLOYEE PROGRAMS

Research Medical Center
2316 E. Meyer Boulevard
Kansas City, MO 64132
(816) 276–4000

Type of Business: Hospital
Type of Child Care: Near or on-site center
# of Employees: 1,980

St. Joseph Hospital
1000 Carondelet Drive
Kansas City, MO 64114
(816) 942–4400

Type of Business: Hospital
Type of Child Care: Near or on-site center
# of Employees: 1,048

St. Joseph Hospital
525 Couch Avenue
Kirkwood, MO 63122
(314) 966–1500

Type of Business: Hospital
Type of Child Care: Near or on-site center
# of Employees: 867

**St. Louis Children's
Hospital**
400 S. King's Highway Blvd.
St. Louis, MO 63110
(314) 454–6000

Type of Business: Hospital
Type of Child Care: Near or on-site center; Financial aid
# of Employees: 1,167

**St. Louis Regional
Medical Center**
5535 Delmar
St. Louis, MO 63112
(314) 879–6308

Type of Business: Hospital
Type of Child Care: Financial aid
# of Employees: 1,407

• • • • • • • • • • • • • • • • • •

St. Luke's Hospital
44th and Wornall Road
Kansas City, MO 64111
(816) 932–2000

Type of Business: Hospital
Type of Child Care: Near or on-site center
# of Employees: 2,995

St. Mary's Health Center
1027 Bellevue Avenue
St. Louis, MO 63117
(314) 781–7400

Type of Business: Hospital
Type of Child Care: Near or on-site center
# of Employees: 1,716

MONTANA

Columbus Hospital
500 15th Avenue, South
Great Falls, MT 59405
(406) 727–3333

Type of Business: Hospital
Type of Child Care: Near or on-site center
# of Employees: 674

Missoula Medical Center
2827 Fort Missoula Road
Missoula, MT 59801
(406) 728–4100

Type of Business: Hospital
Type of Child Care: Near or on-site center
# of Employees: 583

CORPORATE/EMPLOYEE PROGRAMS

. . . .

NEBRASKA

Archbishop Bergan
Mercy Hospital
7500 Mercy Road
Omaha, NE 68124
(402) 398–6763

Type of Business: Hospital
Type of Child Care: Near or on-site center
# of Employees: 1,606

Bryan Memorial Hospital
1600 S. 48th Street
Lincoln, NE 68506
(402) 489–0200

Type of Business: Hospital
Type of Child Care: Near or on-site center
# of Employees: 1,435

Children's Hospital
8301 W. Dodge Road
Omaha, NE 68114
(402) 390–5400

Type of Business: Hospital
Type of Child Care: Near or on-site center
# of Employees: 452

Immanuel Medical Center
6901 N. 72nd Street
Omaha, NE 68122
(402) 572–2121

Type of Business: Hospital
Type of Child Care: Near or on-site center
# of Employees: 1,527

Mutual of Omaha
10235 Regency Circle
Omaha, NE 68114
(402) 397–8555

Type of Business: Insurance
Type of Child Care: On or near-site center
# of Employees: 8,486

Northwestern Bell
1314 Douglas on the Mall
Omaha, NE 68102
(402) 422–2000

Type of Business: Local telephone communications
Type of Child Care: Near-site center
# of Employees: n/a

St. Elizabeth Hospital
555 S. 70th Street
Lincoln, NE 68510
(402) 489–7181

Type of Business: Hospital
Type of Child Care: Near or on-site center
# of Employees: 872

NEVADA

Humana Hospital Sunrise
3816 S. Maryland Parkway
Las Vegas, NV 89109
(702) 731–8000

Type of Business: Hospital
Type of Child Care: Financial aid
# of Employees: 1,921

**Valley Hospital
Medical Center**
620 Shadow Lane
Las Vegas, NV 89109
(702) 388–4000

Type of Business: Hospital
Type of Child Care: Financial aid
# of Employees: 744

CORPORATE/EMPLOYEE PROGRAMS

• • • • • • • • • • • • • • • • • • • •

NEW HAMPSHIRE

Concord Hospital
242 Pleasant Street
Concord, NH 03301
(603) 225–2711

Type of Business: Hospital
Type of Child Care: Near or on-site center
# of Employees: 945

Elliot Hospital
955 Auburn Street
Manchester, NH 03103
(603) 669–5300

Type of Business: Hospital
Type of Child Care: Near or on-site center
# of Employees: 1,019

Hadco Corp.
10 Manor Parkway
Salem, NH 03079
(603) 898–8000

Type of Business: Computer printer circuit manufacture
Type of Child Care: On or near-site center
# of Employees: 1,700

Mary Hitchock Hospital
7 Rope Ferry Road
Hanover, NH 03755
(603) 646–5422

Type of Business: Hospital
Type of Child Care: Financial aid
# of Employees: 2,118

New London Trust Co.
Main Street
P.O. Box 158
New London, NH 03257
(603) 526–2535

Type of Business: Commercial banking
Type of Child Care: On or near-site center
# of Employees: n/a

NEW JERSEY

Bellcore
Bell Communications
Research
290 W. Mount Pleasant Ave.
Livingston, NJ 07039
(201) 740–3297

Type of Business: Research
Type of Child Care: Pretax set-asides; Work–at–home telecommunication program
# of Employees: 8,200

Campbell Soup Co.
Campbell Place
Camden, NJ 081003
(609) 342–4800

Type of Business: Food production
Type of Child Care: On-site child-care center; Summer care program for children up to 3rd grade
# of Employees: 31,000

**East Orange General
Hospital**
300 Central Avenue
East Orange, NJ 07019
(201) 672–8400

Type of Business: Hospital
Type of Child Care: Near or on-site center
# of Employees: 730

**Educational Testing
Service**
Rosedale Road
Princeton, NJ 08540
(609) 921–9000

Type of Business: Educational research & testing
Type of Child Care: Near or on-site center
# of Employees: 2,800

**Hackensack Medical
Center**
214 Terrance Avenue
Hasbrouck, NJ 07604
(201) 288–0800

Type of Business: Hospital
Type of Child Care: Near or on-site center
# of Employees: 2,598

CORPORATE/EMPLOYEE PROGRAMS

- - - - - - - - - - - - - - - - - -

Hoffman – La Roche
340 Kingsland Street
Nutley, NJ 07110
(201) 234–5000

Type of Business: Pharmaceutical manufacture
Type of Child Care: On–site center; Kindergarten; After-school care; Full–time summer program; Emergency and sick care; Pretax set-asides
# of Employees: 17,800

Holy Name Hospital
718 Teaneck Road
Teaneck, NJ 07666
(201) 833–3000

Type of Business: Hospital
Type of Child Care: Near or on-site center
# of Employees: 1,456

Hospital Center at Orange
188 S. Essex Avenue
Orange, NJ 07050
(201) 266–2000

Type of Business: Hospital
Type of Child Care: Near or on-site center
# of Employees: 1,023

Hospital Insurance Plan of New Jersey
Newark, NJ 07101

Type of Business: Insurance, telecommunications conglomerate
Type of Child Care: Near-site center
# of Employees: n/a

John F. Kennedy Medical Center
98 James Street
Edison, NJ 08818
(201) 321–7000

Type of Business: Hospital
Type of Child Care: Near or on-site center
# of Employees: 1,896

• •

Johnson & Johnson
One Johnson &
Johnson Plaza
New Brunswick, NJ 08933
(201) 524–0400

Type of Business: Health care product manufacture
Type of Child Care: Near–site center; Pretax set–asides
# of Employees: 31,000

Mercer Medical Center
Box 1658
Trenton, NJ 08607
(609) 394–4000

Type of Business: Hospital
Type of Child Care: Near or on-site center
# of Employees: 1,247

Mercl & Co.
P.O. Box 2000
Rahway, NJ 07065
(201) 594–4000

Type of Business: Pharmaceutical manufacture
Type of Child Care: Near–site center
# of Employees: 18,700

**Muhlenberg Regional
Medical Center**
Park Avenue & Randolph
South Plainfield, NJ 07061
(201) 668–2000

Type of Business: Hospital
Type of Child Care: Near or on-site center
# of Employees: 1,484

Next Generation, Inc.
Corbett &
Industrial Way West
Eatontown, NJ 07724

Type of Child Care: On or near-site center
# of Employees: n/a

CORPORATE/EMPLOYEE PROGRAMS

Ortho Pharmaceutical Corp.
Route 202
Raritan, NJ 08869
(908) 524–0400

Type of Business: Pharmaceutical manufacture
Type of Child Care: On or near-site center
# of Employees: 2,400

St. Elizabeth Hospital
225 Williamson Street
Elizabeth, NJ 07078
(201) 527–5000

Type of Business: Hospital
Type of Child Care: Near or on-site center
# of Employees: 1,108

St. Francis Hospital
25 McWilliam Place
Jersey City, NJ 07302
(201) 795–7000

Type of Business: Hospital
Type of Child Care: Near or on-site center
# of Employees: 709

St. Mary's Hospital
308 Willow Avenue
Hoboken, NJ 07030
(201) 792–8000

Type of Business: Hospital
Type of Child Care: Near or on-site center
# of Employees: 869

Warner Lambert
201 Tabor Road
Morris Plains, NJ 07950
(201) 540–2000

Type of Business: Pharmaceutical, candy & shaving goods manufacture
Type of Child Care: Near–site center; Pretax set–asides
# of Employees: 10,636

NEW YORK

American Express
American Express Tower
World Financial Center
New York, NY 10285

Type of Business: Travel and financial services
Type of Child Care: Pretax set-asides; Child care costs reimbursed for overtime or travel
# of Employees: 82,459

**American Telephone
& Telegaph**
550 Madison Avenue
New York, NY 10022
(212) 605–5500

Type of Business: Telecommunications and computer sales and service
Type of Child Care: Pretax set-asides; Liberal work–at–home program; Grants to community child–care projects in cities where AT&T employees live
# of Employees: 260,900

Albany Medical Center
New Scotland Avenue
Albany, NY 12208
(518) 445–3125

Type of Business: Hospital
Type of Child Care: Near or on-site center
# of Employees: 3,164

Bellevue Hospital
First Avenue & 27th Street
New York, NY 10016
(212) 561–4141

Type of Business: Hospital
Type of Child Care: Near or on-site center
# of Employees: 5,082

Chemical Bank
277 Park Avenue
New York, NY 10172
(212) 310–6161

Type of Business: Commercial banking
Type of Child Care: Financial aid
# of Employees: n/a

Citibank
399 Park Avenue
New York, NY 10043
(212) 559-1000

Type of Business: Commercial banking
Type of Child Care: On-site centers in Hagerstown, MD & Sioux Falls, SD; Vouchers for child care in some locations; Discounts with child care provides; Pretax set-asides
# of Employees: 56,000

CMP Publications
600 Community Drive
Manhasset, NY 11030
(516) 562-5000

Type of Business: Publishing (periodicals)
Type of Child Care: After-school program; Holiday and summer programs
# of Employees: 1,237

Con Edison
4 Irving Place
New York, NY 10003
(212) 460-4600

Type of Business: Utilities
Type of Child Care: Pretax set-asides; Emergency child-care program
# of Employees: 19,768

Corning
Houghton Park
Corning, NY 14831
(607) 974-9000

Type of Business: Glass and ceramic product manufacture; Clinical testing
Type of Child Care: Near-site center; Pretax set-asides
# of Employees: 20,150

Eastman Kodak Company
343 State Street
Rochester, NY 14650
(716) 724-4000

Type of Business: Photographic equipment manufacture
Type of Child Care: Financial aid
# of Employees: 137,500

Genessee Hospital
224 Alexander Street
Rochester, NY 14607
(716) 263–6000

Type of Business: Hospital
Type of child Care: Near or on-site center
# of Employees: 1,894

**Grummons
Aerospace Corp.**
S. Oyster Bay Road
Bethpage, NY
(516) 575–0574

Type of Business: Aircraft engine & parts production
Type of Child Care: Financial aid
# of Employees: n/a

Grummons Corp.
111 Stewart Avenue
Bethpage, NY 11714
(516) 575–0574

Type of Business: Aircraft research & development;
Defense; Space vehicle parts & equipment manufacture
Type of Child Care: Financial aid
# of Employees: n/a

Home Box Office
1100 Avenue of
the Americas
New York, NY 10036
(212) 512–1113

Type of Business: Subsidiary of Time Warner; Cable
television program production
Type of Child Care: Pretax set–asides; Emergency child
care; Child care costs reimbursed for overtime or travel
# of Employees: 728

**Hudson River
Psychiatric Center**
Branch B
Poughkeepsie, NY 12601
(914) 452–8000

Type of Business: Hospital
Type of Child Care: Near or on-site center
# of Employees: 1,348

CORPORATE/EMPLOYEE PROGRAMS

• • • • • • • • • • • • • • • • • • •

Hutchings Psychiatric Center
620 Madison Street
Syracuse, NY 13210
(315) 473–4980

Type of Business: Hospital
Type of Child Care: Near or on-site center
# of Employees: 854

IBM
2000 Purchase Street
Purchase, NY 10577
(914) 697–7100

Type of Business: Computer manufacture
Type of Child Care: $25 million fund for child care/ elder care over next five years
# of Employees: 216,000

Kings Park Psychiatric Center
Box 9000
Kings Park, NY 11754
(516) 544–2957

Type of Business: Hospital
Type of Child Care: Near or on-site center
# of Employees: 3,151

Lederle Laboratories
61 Convent Road
Nanyet, NY 10954

Type of Child Care: On or near-site center
# of Employees: n/a

Lourdes Hospital
169 Riverside Drive
Binghamton, NY 12905
(607) 798–5111

Type of Business: Hospital
Type of Child Care: On–site center; Pretax set-asides
# of Employees: 1,520

• • • • • • • • • • • • • • • • • • • •

Merrill Lynch
2 Broadway
New York, NY 10004
(212) 449,1000

Type of Business: Stock brokerage
Type of Child Care: Financial aid
# of Employees: 41,000

Methodist Hospital
of Brooklyn
506 6th Street
Brooklyn, NY 11215
(718) 780–3000

Type of Business: Hospital
Type of Child Care: Near or on-site center
# of Employees: 2,086

Middletown Psychiatric
Center
P.O. Box 1453
Middletown, NY 10940
(914) 343–2424

Type of Business: Hospital
Type of Child Care: Near or on-site center
# of Employees: 1,176

Morgan Guaranty Trust
23 Wall Street
New York, NY 10015
(212) 483–2323

Type of Business: Financial services
Type of Child Care: Financial aid
# of Employees: 12,000

Mt. Sinai Hospital
1 Gustave L. Levy Place
New York, NY 10029
(212) 241–6500

Type of Business: Hospital
Type of Child Care: Near or on-site center
# of Employees: 6,031

CORPORATE/EMPLOYEE PROGRAMS

• • • • • • • • • • • • • • • • • • •

Pilgrim Psychiatric Center
West Brentwood, NY 11717
(516) 434–7500

Type of Business: Hospital
Type of Child Care: Near or on-site center
# of Employees: 3,484

St. Luke's –
Roosevelt Hospital
428 W. 59th Street
New York, NY 10019
(212) 523–4000

Type of Business: Hospital
Type of Child Care: Near or on-site center
# of Employees: n/a

Roswell Park
Cancer Institute
Elm & Carlton
Buffalo, NY 14263
(716) 845–2300

Type of Business: Hospital
Type of Child Care: Near or on-site center
# of Employees: 1,353

United Nations
Development Corp.
2 U.N. Plaza
New York, NY 10017
(212) 702–5100

Type of Business: Subdividing and development
Type of Child Care: On or near-site center
# of Employees: n/a

NORTH CAROLINA

Acme McCrary
P.O. Box 1287
Asheboro, NC 27203
(919) 625-2161

Type of Business: Women's hosiery manufacture
Type of Child Care: Near or on-site center
# of Employees: 900

Alamance County Hospital
P.O. Box 202
Burlington, NC 27216
(919) 228-1371

Type of Business: Hospital
Type of Child Care: Near or on-site center
# of Employees: 531

Burroughs Wellcome Company
3030 Cornwalls Road
Triangle Park, NC 27609
(919) 248-3000

Type of Business: Pharmaceutical manufacture
Type of Child Care: Financial aid
# of Employees: 4,600

NCNB
One NCNB Plaza
Charlotte, NC 28255
(704) 374-5000

Type of Business: Commercial banking
Type of Child Care: Pretax set-asides; Child care subsidies; (now building a near-site center)
# of Employees: 28,800

Neuville Industries, Inc.
P.O. Box 286
Hildebran, NC 28637
(704) 397-5560

Type of Business: Clothing manufacture
Type of Child Care: On or near-site center
# of Employees: 500

CORPORATE/EMPLOYEE PROGRAMS

• • • • • • • • • • • • • • • • • • •

Presbyterian Hospital
P.O. Box 33549
Charlotte, NC 28233
(704) 371–4000

Type of Business: Hospital
Type of Child Care: Near or on-site center
# of Employees: 2,943

Rex Hospital
4420 Lake Boone Trail
Raleigh, NC 27607
(919) 783–3100

Type of Business: Hospital
Type of Child Care: Near or on-site center
# of Employees: 1,731

SAS Institute, Inc.
SAS Campus Drive
Cary, NC 27513
(919) 677–8000

Type of Business: Computer software production
Type of Child Care: On–site centers; Pretax set–asides
# of Employees: 1,428

United States Hosiery
P.O. Box 160
Lincolnton, NC 28092
(704) 735–3041

Type of Business: Hosiery manufacture
Type of Child Care: On–site center
# of Employees: 282

. . . .

NORTH DAKOTA

**North Dakota State
Hospital**
Box 476
Jamestown, ND 58401
(701) 253–3650

Type of Business: Hospital
Type of Child Care: Near or on-site center
# of Employees: 699

**St. Luke's Hospitals –
Meritcare**
720 4th Street, North
Fargo, ND 58122
(701) 234–5100

Type of Business: Hospital
Type of Child Care: Near or on-site center
# of Employees: 1,426

OHIO

Akron City Hospital
525 E. Market Street
Akron, OH 44309
(216) 375–3000

Type of Business: Hospital
Type of Child Care: Near or on-site center
# of Employees: 2,667

Bethesda Oak Hospital
619 Oak Street
Cincinnati, OH 45206
(513) 569–6111

Type of Business: Hospital
Type of Child Care: Near or on-site center
# of Employees: 1,884

CORPORATE/EMPLOYEE PROGRAMS

. . . .

**Children's Hospital
Medical Center**
1 Children's Plaza
Dayton, OH 45404
(513) 226–8300

Type of Business: Hospital
Type of Child Care: Near or on-site center
# of Employees: 1,064

Cleveland Clinic
9500 Euclid Avenue
Cleveland, OH 44106
(216) 444–2200

Type of Business: Hospital
Type of Child Care: Financial aid
# of Employees: 4,811

Grant Medical Center
111 S. Grant
Columbus, OH 43215
(614) 461–3232

Type of Business: Hospital
Type of Child Care: Financial aid
# of Employees: 1,715

Little Tykes
(Rubbermaid subsidiary)
21800 Barlow Road
Hudson, OH 44236
(216) 650–3000

Type of Business: Pre–school toy manufacture
Type of Child Care: On–site center; After–school program for kindergarten
# of Employees: 1,450

Mead Data Central
9443 Springsboro Pike
Dayton, OH 45342
(513) 865–6800

Type of Business: Computerized legal, accounting and news research service
Type of Child Care: On or near-site center
# of Employees: 3,299

Mercy Hospital
2200 Jefferson Avenue
Toledo, OH 43624
(419) 259–1500

Type of Business: Hospital
Type of Child Care: Near or on-site center
# of Employees: 1,143

Miami Valley Hospital
1 Wyoming Street
Dayton, OH 45410
(513) 223–6192

Type of Business: Hospital
Type of Child Care: Financial aid
# of Employees: 2,520

Mount Carmel Medical Center
793 W. State Street
Columbus, OH 43213
(614) 868–6000

Type of Business: Hospital
Type of Child Care: Financial aid
# of Employees: 2,917

Proctor & Gamble
One Proctor &
Gamble Plaza
Cincinnati, OH 45202
(513) 983–1100

Type of Business: Household products manufacture
Type of Child Care: Near–site centers; Pretax set–asides
# of Employees: 43,600

Providence Hospital
2446 Kipling Avenue
Cincinnati, OH 45239
(513) 853–5249

Type of Business: Hospital
Type of Child Care: Near or on-site center
# of Employees: 1,171

CORPORATE/EMPLOYEE PROGRAMS

• • • • • • • • • • • • • • • • • • • •

Providence Hospital
1912 Hayes Avenue
Sandusky, OH 44870
(419) 625–8450

Type of Business: Hospital
Type of Child Care: Near or on-site center
# of Employees: 632

Riverside Hospital
1600 Superior Street
Toledo, OH 43604
(419) 729–6000

Type of Business: Hospital
Type of Child Care: Near or on-site center
# of Employees: 806

**Riverside Methodist
Hospital**
3535 Olentangy River Road
Columbus, OH 43214
(614) 261–5000

Type of Business: Hospital
Type of Child Care: Near or on-site center
# of Employees: 4,104

**St. Vincent's
Medical Center**
2213 Cherry Street
Toledo, OH 43608
(419) 321–3232

Type of Business: Hospital
Type of Child Care: Near or on-site center
# of Employees: 2,545

Toledo Hospital
2142 N. Cover Boulevard
Toledo, OH 43606
(419) 471–4218

Type of Business: Hospital
Type of Child Care: Near or on-site center
# of Employees: 3,825

OKLAHOMA

Bank of Oklahoma
1 William Center
Tulsa, OK 74172
(918) 588–6000

Type of Business: Commercial banking
Type of Child Care: Financial aid
# of Employees: 1,170

Baptist Medical Center
3300 N. W. Expressway
Oklahoma City, OK 73112
(405) 949–3011

Type of Business: Hospital
Type of Child Care: Near or on-site center
# of Employees: 2,642

Hillcrest Medical Center
1120 S. Utica Street
Tulsa, OK 74104
(918) 587–1300

Type of Business: Hospital
Type of Child Care: Near or on-site center
# of Employees: 1,555

Mercy Hospital
4300 W. Memorial Road
Oklahoma City, OK 73120
(405) 755–1515

Type of Business: Hospital
Type of Child Care: Near or on-site center
# of Employees: 1,198

Muskogee Regional Medical Center
300 Rockefeller Drive
Muskogee, OK 74401
(918) 682–5501

Type of Business: Hospital
Type of Child Care: Near or on-site center
# of Employees: 884

CORPORATE/EMPLOYEE PROGRAMS

. . . .

St. Francis Hospital
6161 S. Yale
Tulsa, OK 74117
(918) 494–2200

Type of Business: Hospital
Type of Child Care: Near or on-site center
# of Employees: 3,310

St. John's Medical Center
1923 S. Utica
Tulsa, OK 74104
(918) 744–2345

Type of Business: Hospital
Type of Child Care: Near or on-site center; Financial aid
# of Employees: 2,818

OREGON

Good Samaritan Hospital
1015 N. W. 22nd Avenue
Portland, OR 97210
(503) 229–7711

Type of Business: Hospital
Type of Child Care: Financial aid
# of Employees: 2,023

Holladay Park Hospital
1225 N.E. Second Avenue
Portland, OR 97212
(503) 233–4567

Type of Business: Hospital
Type of Child Care: Near or on-site center
# of Employees: 401

PENNSYLVANIA

**Abington Memorial
Hospital**
1200 Old York Road
Abington, PA 19001
(215) 576–2009

Type of Business: Hospital
Type of Child Care: Near or on-site center
# of Employees: 2,128

**Allegheny International,
Inc.**
2 Oliver Plaza
Pittsburgh, PA 15230
(412) 526–4000

Type of Business: Small appliance manufacture
Type of Child Care: On or near-site center
# of Employees: 12,000

**Aluminum Co. of America
(Alcoa)**
1501 Alcoa Building
Pittsburgh, PA 15219
(412) 553–4545

Type of Company: Aluminum manufacture
Type of Child Care: On or near-site center
# of Employees: 60,600

**Amalgamated Clothing &
Textile Workers Union**
Chambersburg, PA 17201

Type of Business: Textile union
Type of Child Care: On or near-site center
# of Employees: n/a

Black Box Corporation
Mayview and Park Drive
Pittsburgh, PA 15241

Type of Business: Peripheral computer equipment
manufacture
Type of Child Care: Financial aid
# of Employees: 600

CORPORATE/EMPLOYEE PROGRAMS

. . . .

Carpenter Technology Corporation
101 W. Bern Street
Reading, PA 19601
(215) 371–2000

Type of Business: Steel manufacture
Type of Child Care: Financial aid
# of Employees: 3,540

Colonial Penn Service Corp.
Colonial Penn Plaza, 19th
and Market Streets
Philadelphia, PA 19181
(215) 988–8000

Type of Business: Insurance
Type of Child Care: Financial aid
# of Employees: 425

The Kevin F. Donohoe Co.
Rocking Horse Child Care
Centers of America
Independence Square
Philadelphia, PA 19106

Type of Child Care: On or near-site center
# of Employees: n/a

Doylestown Hospital
595 W. State Street
Doylestown, PA 18901
(215) 345–2000

Type of Business: Hospital
Type of Child Care: Near or on-site center
# of Employees: 1,030

Dravo
1 Oliver Plaza
Pittsburgh, PA 15230
(412) 566–3000

Type of Business: Concrete manufacture
Type of Child Care: Near-site center
# of Employees: 2,456

The Fox Co.
Rocking Horse Child Care
Centers of America
Wayne, PA 19087

Type of Child Care: On or near-site center
# of Employees: n/a

Frankford Hospital
Frankford Avenue &
Wakeling Street
Philadelphia, PA 19124
(215) 831–2000

Type of Business: Hospital
Type of Child Care: Near or on-site center
# of Employees: 1,531

Globe–Weis
Wood Avenue & Cherry St.
Bristol, PA 15007

Type of Child Care: On-site center
# of Employees: n/a

Hartsbrings, Inc.
270 E. Conestoga Road
Stratford, PA 19087
(215) 687–6900

Type of Business: Children's apparel manufacture
Type of Child Care: On or near-site center
# of Employees: n/a

Hatfield Packing Co.
Hatfield Quality Meats, Inc.
Hatfield, PA 15440
(215) 368–2500

Type of Business: Pork products manufacture
Type of Child Care: On or near-site center
# of Employees: n/a

CORPORATE/EMPLOYEE PROGRAMS

. . . .

Institute for Scientific Information
3501 Market Street
Philadelphia, PA 19104
(215) 386–0100

Type of Business: Publishing (periodicals); Information retrieval service; Investment advising service
Type of Child Care: On or near-site center
# of Employees: n/a

Korman Co.
Just Children Child
Development Centers
Trevose, PA 19047

Type of Child Care: On or near-site centers
# of Employees: n/a

Lancaster Laboratories
2425 New Holland Pike
Lancaster, PA 17601
(717) 656–2301

Type of Business: Clinical testing
Type of Child Care: On–site center; After-school care; Summer day camp; Pretax set–asides
# of Employees: 365

Mercy Hospital
1400 Locust Street
Pittsburgh, PA 15219
(412) 232–8111

Type of Business: Hospital
Type of Child Care: Near or on-site center
# of Employees: 2,279

Mercy Hospital
2500 7th Avenue
Altoona, PA 16608
(814) 944–1681

Type of Business: Hospital
Type of Child Care: Near or on-site center
# of Employees: 630

Presbyterian University Hospital
DeSota and O'Hara Streets
Pittsburg, PA 15213
(412) 647-3014

Type of Business: Hospital
Type of Child Care: Near or on-site center
# of Employees: 3,549

Private Industry Council
1601 Union Boulevard
Allentown, PA 18101

Type of Child Care: On or near-site center
# of Employees: n/a

Reading Hospital and Medical Center
6th and Spruce
W. Reading, PA 19603
(215) 378-6000

Type of Business: Hospital
Type of Child Care: Near or on-site center
# of Employees: 2,345

St. Luke's Hospital
Schoenersville Road
Bethlehem, PA 18017
(215) 861-2200

Type of Business: Hospital
Type of Child Care: Near or on-site center
# of Employees: 1,585

St. Vincent Health Center
232 W. 25th Street
Erie, PA 16544
(814) 452-5000

Type of Business: Hospital
Type of Child Care: Near or on-site center
# of Employees: 1,995

CORPORATE/EMPLOYEE PROGRAMS

• • • • • • • • • • • • • • • • • • • •

**Union Fidelity Life
Insurance**
4850 Street Road, Rte. 132
Trevose, PA 19047
(215) 953–3000

Type of Business: Insurance
Type of Child Care: On or near-site center
# of Employees: n/a

**Western Pennsylvania
Hospital**
4800 Friendship Avenue
Pittsburgh, PA 15224
(412) 478–5000

Type of Business: Hospital
Type of Child Care: Near or on-site center; Financial aid
# of Employees: 2,331

RHODE ISLAND

**Allendale
Life Insurance Co.**
1301 Atwood Avenue
Johnston, RI 02919
(401) 275–3000

Type of Business: Insurance
Type of Child Care: On or near-site center
# of Employees: 1,214

**Opportunities
Industrialization Center
of Rhode Island**
1 Hilton Street
Providence, RI 02905

Type of Child Care: On or near-site center
# of Employees: n/a

• • • • • • • • • • • • • • • • • • • •

SOUTH CAROLINA

Greenville News Piedmont
P.O. Box 1688
Greenville, SC 29602

Type of Business: Newspaper
Type of Child Care: On or near-site center
# of Employees: n/a

**McLeod Regional
Medical Center**
555 E. Cheves Street
Florence, SC 29501
(808) 667–2000

Type of Business: Hospital
Type of Child Care: Near or on-site center
# of Employees: 1,690

**Spartanburg Regional
Medical Center**
Box 3217
Spartanburg, SC 29304
(803) 573–3000

Type of Business: Hospital
Type of Child Care: Near or on-site center
# of Employees: 2,403

SOUTH DAKOTA

Sacred Heart Hospital
501 Summit
Yankton, SD 57073
(605) 665–9371

Type of Business: Hospital
Type of Child Care: Near or on-site center
# of Employees: 438

CORPORATE/EMPLOYEE PROGRAMS

. . . .

St. Luke's Hospital
305 S. State Street
Aberdeen, SD 57401
(605) 622–5000

Type of Business: Hospital
Type of Child Care: Near or on-site center
# of Employees: 776

Sioux Valley Hospital
1100 S. Euclid Street
Sioux Falls, SD 57117
(605) 333–1000

Type of Business: Hospital
Type of Child Care: Near or on-site center
# of Employees: 2,309

TENNESSEE

Baptist Memorial Hospital
6019 Walnut Grove Road
Memphis, TN 38119
(901) 766–5000

Type of Business: Hospital
Type of Child Care: Near or on-site center
# of Employees: 5,866

Dede Wallace Institute
2200 Hillsboro Road
Nashville, TN 37212

Type of Child Care: On or near-site center
# of Employees: n/a

**Fort Sanders Regional
Medical Center**
1901 Clinch Avenue, SW
Knoxville, TN 37916
(615) 541–1111

Type of Business: Hospital
Type of Child Care: Near or on-site center
# of Employees: 1,925

Hospital Corp. of America
Park Plaza
Nashville, TN 37202
(615) 327–9551

Type of Business: Hospital ownership/management
Type of Child Care: Near or on-site center
# of Employees: 60,000

**Jackson Madison
County Hospital**
708 W. Forest Avenue
Jackson, TN 38301
(901) 425–5000

Type of Business: Hospital
Type of Child Care: Financial aid
# of Employees: 2,054

Memorial Hospital
2525 DeSalles Avenue
Chattanooga, TN 37404
(615) 495–2525

Type of Business: Hospital
Type of Child Care: Near or on-site center
# of Employees: 1,266

Opryland, USA
2801 Opryland Drive
Nashville, TN 37214
(615) 321–5000

Type of Business: Entertainment park and hotel
Type of Child Care: On or near-site center
# of Employees: 3,500

St. Mary's Medical Center
Oak Hill Avenue
Knoxville, TN 37917
(615) 971–6011

Type of Business: Hospital
Type of Child Care: Near or on-site center
# of Employees: 1,823

St. Thomas Hospital
4220 Harding Road
Nashville, TN 37205
(615) 386–2111

Type of Business: Hospital
Type of Child Care: Near or on-site center; Financial aid
# of Employees: 2,753

TEXAS

American Airlines
P.O. Box 619616
Dallas/Ft. Worth Airport
Dallas/Ft. Worth 75261
(817) 936–1234

Type of Business: Airline
Type of Child Care: On or near-site center
# of Employees: 77,000

Baylor University Medical Center
3500 Gaston Avenue
Dallas, TX 75246
(214) 820–0111

Type of Business: Hospital
Type of Child Care: Near or on-site center
# of Employees: 3,912

• • • • • • • • • • • • • • • • • • •

Compaq Computer Corp.
P.O. Box 69–2000
Houston, TX 77269
(713) 370–0670

Type of Business: Personal/portable computer manufacture
Type of Child Care: Financial aid
# of Employees: 9,500

**Dr. Pepper – 7–Up
Companies**
P.O. Box 655086
Dallas, TX 75265
(214) 360–7000

Type of Business: Soft drink manufacture
Type of Child Care: Near-site center
# of Employees: 842

**Harris County
Hospital District**
1502 Taub Loop
Houston, TX 77030
(713) 793–2000

Type of Business: Hospital
Type of Child Care: Near-site center
# of Employees: 3,728

**Harris Methodist
Fort Worth Hospital**
1301 Pennsylvania Avenue
Fort Worth, TX 76104
(817) 882–2000

Type of Business: Hospital
Type of Child Care: Near or on site center; Financial aid
# of Employees: 2,345

Hermann Hospital
6411 Fannin
Houston, TX 77030
(713) 797–4011

Type of Business: Hospital
Type of Child Care: Near-site center
# of Employees: 2,724

CORPORATE/EMPLOYEE PROGRAMS

•   •   •   •   •   •   •   •   •   •   •   •   •   •   •   •   •   •   •

High Plains Baptist Hospital
1600 Wallace Boulevard
Amarillo, TX 79106
(806) 358–3151

Type of Business: Hospital
Type of Child Care: Near or on-site center
# of Employees: 1,040

Lomas Nettleton Mortgage Investors
1600 Viceroy
Dallas, TX 75235
(214) 746–7111

Type of Business: Mortgage loan investment
Type of Child Care: On or near-site center
# of Employees: 9

LTV Corporation
P.O. Box 655003
Dallas, TX 75265
(214) 979–7711

Type of Business: Defense; Steel production; Energy products manufacture
Type of Child Care: Financial aid
# of Employees: 38,000

Memorial Medical Center
P.O. Box 5280
Corpus Christi, TX 78405
(512) 881–4000

Type of Business: Hospital
Type of Child Care: Near or on-site center
# of Employees: 1,145

Methodist Hospital
6565 Fannin
Houston, TX 77030
(713) 790–3311

Type of Business: Hospital
Type of Child Care: Near-site center
# of Employees: 5,925

. . . .

**Presbyterian Hospital
of Dallas**
8200 Walnut Hill Lane
Dallas, TX 75237
(214) 369–4111

Type of Business: Hospital
Type of Child Care: Near or on-site center
# of Employees: 2,718

St. Luke's Hospital
Box 20269
Houston, TX 77225
(713) 791–2011

Type of Business: Hospital
Type of Child Care: Near-site center
# of Employees: 3,801

St. Paul Medical Center
5909 Harry Hines Boulevard
Dallas, TX 75235
(214) 879–1000

Type of Business: Hospital
Type of Child Care: Near or on-site center
# of Employees: 1,735

Seton Medical Center
1201 W. 38th Street
Austin, TX 78705
(512) 323–1900

Type of Business: Hospital
Type of Child Care: Financial aid
# of Employees: 1,937

**Super Sack
Manufacturing Corp.**
Savoy Lane &
Recreation Center
P.O. Box 444
Savoy, TX 75479

Type of Child Care: On and off-site centers
# of Employees: n/a

· · · · · · · · · · · · · · · · · ·

Tandy Corp.
500 One Tandy Center
Ft. Worth, TX 76102
(817) 390–3700

Type of Business: Consumer electronics
Type of Child Care: On or near-site center
# of Employees: 32,000

Tenneco
P.O. Box 2511
Houston, TX 77252
(713) 757–2131

Type of Business: Shipping; Construction; Farm machinery manufacture
Type of Child Care: Pretax set–asides; Subsidized sick child care; Child care costs reimbursement for overtime or travel
# of Employees: 85,000

Texas Children's Hospital
6621 Fannin Street
Houston, TX 77030
(713) 798–1000

Type of Business: Hospital
Type of Child Care: Near-site center
# of Employees: 1,575

Trammell Crow Company
2001 Ross Avenue
Dallas, TX 75201
(214) 979–5100

Type of Business: Real estate development
Type of Child Care: Near–site center; Summer program; Pretax set–asides
# of Employees: 3,400

Zales Corp.
P.O. Box 15277
Irving, TX 75015
(214) 580–4000

Type of Business: Retail jewelry sales
Type of Child Care: On or near-site center
# of Employees: 12,700

UTAH

Conant Associates
215 S. State
Salt Lake City, UT 84011

Type of Child Care: On and off-site centers
# of Employees: n/a

Judkins Company
2550 S.W. Temple
Salt Lake City, UT 84115

Type of Child Care: On and off-site centers
# of Employees: n/a

Sperry Corp.
322 N. Sperry Way
Salt Lake City, UT 84116

Type of Business: Shoe manufacture
Type of Child Care: Financial aid
# of Employees: n/a

Utah State Hospital
1300 E. Center Street
Provo, UT 84603
(801) 373-4400

Type of Business: Hospital
Type of Child Care: Near or on-site center
# of Employees: 529

Utah Valley Regional Medical Center
1034 N. 500 West
Provo, UT 84603
(801) 373-7850

Type of Business: Hospital
Type of Child care: Near or on-site center
# of Employees: 1,533

CORPORATE/EMPLOYEE PROGRAMS

• • • • • • • • • • • • • • • • • • •

VERMONT

Oliver Wight Companies
5 Oliver Wight Drive
Essex Junction, VT 05452

Type of Child Care: On and off-site centers; Financial aid
# of Employees: n/a

VIRGINIA

Arlington Hospital
1701 N. George Mason Dr.
Arlington, VA 22205
(703) 558–5000

Type of Business: Hospital
Type of Child Care: Near or on-site center
# of Employees: 1,352

**Community Hospital
of Roanoke**
P.O. Box 12946
Roanoke, VA 24029
(703) 985–8000

Type of Business: Hospital
Type of Child Care: Near or on-site center
# of Employees: 1,115

Dominion Bankshares
P.O. Box 13327
Roanoke, VA 24040
(703) 563–7909

Type of Business: Commercial banking
Type of Child Care: On–site center; Pretax set–asides
# of Employees: 6,164

Gannett
1100 Wilson Boulevard
Arlington, VA 22234
(703) 284–6000

Type of Business: Communications conglomerate
Type of Child Care: Pretax set-asides
# of Employees: 37,000

Halmode Apparel Inc.
2820 Ridge Field Street, NE
Roanoake, VA 24012

Type of Business: Women's & children's apparel manufacture
Type of Child Care: On and off-site centers
# of Employees: n/a

Halmode Apparel Inc.
728 Wertz Road, NE
Roanoke, VA 24012
(703) 563–2801

Mount Vernon Hospital
2501 Parker Lane
Alexandria, VA 22306
(703) 664–7000

Type of Business: Hospital
Type of Child Care: Near or on-site center
# of Employees: 764

Roanoke Memorial Hospital
Belleview at Jefferson
Roanoke, VA 24011
(703) 981–7000

Type of Business: Hospital
Type of child Care: Near or on-site center
# of Employees: 2,227

CORPORATE/EMPLOYEE PROGRAMS

• • • • • • • • • • • • • • • • • • •

Rockwell
Charles E. Smith Co.
Patent & Trademark Office
U.S.Air
2345 Crystal Drive
Arlington, VA 22202
(703) 920–8500

Type of Child Care: Off-site center
# of Employees: n/a

**University of Virginia
Hospital**
P.O. Box 2
Charlottesville, VA 22901
(804) 924–8787

Type of Business: Hospital
Type of Child Care: Near or on-site center
# of Employees: 1,028

Virginia Baptist Hospital
3300 Rivermont Avenue
Lynchburg, VA 24503
(804) 522–4000

Type of Business: Hospital
Type of Child Care: Near or on-site center
# of Employees: 1,028

WASHINGTON

Carver Corp.
P.O. Box 1237
Lynwood, WA 98046
(206) 775–1202

Type of Business: High-fidelity audio systems manufacture
Type of Child Care: On or near-site center
# of Employees: n/a

• • • • • • • • • • • • • • • • • • •

Deaconess Hospital
800 W. 5th Avenue
Spokane, WA 99120
(509) 458–7100

Type of Business: Hospital
Type of Child Care: Near or on-site center
# of Employees: 1,348

Northwest Hospital
1550 W. 115th Avenue
Seattle, WA 89133
(206) 364–0500

Type of Business: Hospital
Type of Child Care: Near or on-site center
# of Employees: 1,119

St. Joseph's Hospital
P.O. Box 2197
Tacoma, WA 98401
(206) 627–4101

Type of Business: Hospital
Type of child Care: Near or on-site center
# of Employees: 1,769

Tacoma General Hospital
P.O. Box 5299
Tacoma, WA 98405
(206) 594–1000

Type of Business: Hospital
Type of Child Care: Near or on-site center
# of Employees: 1,581

**Virginia Mason
Medical Center**
925 Seneca Street
Seattle, WA 98101
(206) 624–1144

Type of Business: Hospital
Type of Child Care: Near or on-site center
# of Employees: 1,324

• • • • • • • • • • • • • • • • • • •

WEST VIRGINIA

Charleston Area
Medical Center
P.O. Box 1393
Charleston, WV 25325
(304) 348–5432

Type of Business: Hospital
Type of Child Care: Near or on-site center
# of Employees: 3,187

WISCONSIN

Johnson Wax
1525 Howe Street
Racine, WI 53403
(414) 631–2000

Type of Business: Household products manufacture
Type of Child Care: Near–site center; Summer day camp
# of Employees: 3,350

Luther Hospital
1221 Whipple Street
Eau Claire, WI 54702
(715) 839–3311

Type of Business: Hospital
Type of child Care: Near or on-site center
# of Employees: 769

Marquette Electronics
8200 W. Tower Avenue
Milwaukee, WI 53223
(414) 355–5000

Type of Business: Electrocardiograph manufacture; Patient monitoring systems manufacture; Medical equipment rental
Type of Child Care: On and off-site centers
# of Employees: n/a

. . . .

St. Agnes Hospital
430 E. Division Street
Fond Du Lac, WI 54935
(414) 929–2300

Type of Business: Hospital
Type of Child Care: Near or on-site center
# of Employees: 845

St. Elizabeth Hospital
1506 S. Oneida Street
Appleton, WI 54915
(414) 738–2000

Type of Business: Hospital
Type of Child Care: Financial aid
# of Employees: 950

St. Francis Hospital
3237 S. 16th Street
Milwaukee, WI 53215
(414) 647–5000

Type of Business: Hospital
Type of Child Care: Financial aid
# of Employees: 911

St. Luke's Medical Center
2900 W. Oklahoma Avenue
Milwaukee, WI 53215
(414) 649–6000

Type of Business: Hospital
Type of Child Care: Near or on-site center
# of Employees: 2,199

St. Mary's Hospital
2323 N. Lake Drive
Milwaukee, WI 53211
(414) 225–8000

Type of Business: Hospital
Type of Child Care: Financial aid
# of Employees: 1,328

CORPORATE/EMPLOYEE PROGRAMS

• • • • • • • • • • • • • • • • • •

St. Vincent Hospital
P.O. Box 13508
Green Bay, WI 54307
(414) 433–0111

Type of Business: Hospital
Type of Child Care: Near or on-site center
# of Employees: 1,503

**Waukesha Memorial
Hospital**
725 American Way
Waukesha, WI 53188
(414) 544–2011

Type of Business: Hospital
Type of Child Care: Near or on-site center
# of Employees: 865

Volunteer Program Funding

(Within each state, local families and their children may apply)

• •

The following chapter lists funding sources for volunteer-staffed community day care programs on a state-by-state basis. The common element of these projects is that volunteers offer time to match government dollars awarded to community day care projects. For further information on these programs, please contact the national Technical Assistance Officer in Washington, D.C. at (202) 634-9757, or telephone the local contact listed.

VOLUNTEER PROGRAM FUNDING

• •

ALABAMA

**Alabama Minigrant
Program**
ACTION
600 Beacon Parkway West,
Room 770
Birmingham, AL 35209
(205) 731-1908

Description: Funding to establish local community
projects, such as day-care centers, that encourage
volunteerism; monies awarded must be matched by
volunteer participation
$ Given: $500 to $10,000 per award
Requirements: Project volunteers must participate 1/2
hour for every dollar awarded
Contact: John Timmons

ALASKA

Alaska Minigrant Program
ACTION
909 First Avenue,
Suite 3039
Seattle, WA 98174
(206) 442-1558

Description: Funding to establish local community
projects, such as day-care centers, that encourage
volunteerism; monies awarded must be matched by
volunteer participation
$ Given: $500 to $10,000 per award
Requirements: Project volunteers must participate 1/2
hour for every dollar awarded
Contact: Devin Carroll

ARIZONA

**Arizona Minigrant
Program**
ACTION
522 North Central,
Room 205-A
Phoenix, AZ 85004
(602) 261-4825

Description: Funding to establish local community
projects, such as day-care centers, that encourage
volunteerism; monies awarded must be matched by
volunteer participation
$ Given: $500 to $10,000 per award
Requirements: Project volunteers must participate 1/2
hour for every dollar awarded
Contact: Jess Sixkiller

. . . .

ARKANSAS

**Arkansas Minigrant
Program**
ACTION
700 West Capitol Street
Little Rock, AR 72201
(501) 378-5234

Description: Funding to establish local community
projects, such as day-care centers, that encourage
volunteerism; monies awarded must be matched by
volunteer participation
$ Given: $500 to $10,000 per award
Requirements: Project volunteers must participate 1/2
hour for every dollar awarded
Contact: Robert Torvestad

CALIFORNIA

**California Minigrant
Program**
ACTION
1100 Wilshire Boulevard,
Room 14218
Los Angeles, CA 90024
(213) 209-7421

Description: Funding to establish local community
projects, such as day-care centers, that encourage
volunteerism; monies awarded must be matched by
volunteer participation
$ Given: $500 to $10,000 per award
Requirements: Project volunteers must participate 1/2
hour for every dollar awarded
Contact: Ricardo Gerakos

COLORADO

**Colorado Minigrant
Program**
ACTION
1845 Sherman Street,
Room 301
Denver, CO 80203
(303) 866-1070

Description: Funding to establish local community
projects, such as day-care centers, that encourage
volunteerism; monies awarded must be matched by
volunteer participation
$ Given: $500 to $10,000 per award
Requirements: Project volunteers must participate 1/2
hour for every dollar awarded
Contact: Ben Knopp

VOLUNTEER PROGRAM FUNDING

• •

CONNECTICUT

**Connecticut Minigrant
Program**
ACTION
Ribicoff Federal Building
450 Main Street, Room 524
Hartford, CT 06103
(203) 240-3237

Description: Funding to establish local community projects, such as day-care centers, that encourage volunteerism; monies awarded must be matched by volunteer participation
$ Given: $500 to $10,000 per award
Requirements: Project volunteers must participate 1/2 hour for every dollar awarded
Contact: Romero A. Cherry

DELAWARE

**Delaware Minigrant
Program**
ACTION
31 Hopkins Plaza,
Room 1125
Baltimore, MD 21201
(301) 962-4443

Description: Funding to establish local community projects, such as day-care centers, that encourage volunteerism; monies awarded must be matched by volunteer participation
$ Given: $500 to $10,000 per award
Requirements: Project volunteers must participate 1/2 hour for every dollar awarded
Contact: Jerry Yates

FLORIDA

Florida Minigrant Program
ACTION
3165 McCrory Street,
Suite 115
Orlando, FL 32803
(407) 648-6117

Description: Funding to establish local community projects, such as day-care centers, that encourage volunteerism; monies awarded must be matched by volunteer participation
$ Given: $500 to $10,000 per award
Requirements: Project volunteers must participate 1/2 hour for every dollar awarded
Contact: Henry Jibaja

GEORGIA

Georgia Minigrant Program
ACTION
75 Piedmont Avenue, NE,
Suite 412
Atlanta, GA 30303
(404) 841-4646

Description: Funding to establish local community projects, such as day-care centers, that encourage volunteerism; monies awarded must be matched by volunteer participation
$ Given: $500 to $10,000 per award
Requirements: Project volunteers must participate 1/2 hour for every dollar awarded
Contact: David Dammann

HAWAII

Hawaii Minigrant Program
ACTION
Federal Building, No. 6326
P.O. Box 50024
Honolulu, HI 96850
(808) 541-2832

Description: Funding to establish local community projects, such as day-care centers, that encourage volunteerism; monies awarded must be matched by volunteer participation
$ Given: $500 to $10,000 per award
Requirements: Project volunteers must participate 1/2 hour for every dollar awarded
Contact: Michael Gale

IDAHO

Idaho Minigrant Program
ACTION
1020 Main Street, Suite 340
Boise, ID 83702
(208) 334-1707

Description: Funding to establish local community projects, such as day-care centers, that encourage volunteerism; monies awarded must be matched by volunteer participation
$ Given: $500 to $10,000 per award
Requirements: Project volunteers must participate 1/2 hour for every dollar awarded
Contact: Wilford Overgard

VOLUNTEER PROGRAM FUNDING

• • • • • • • • • • • • • • • • • • • •

ILLINOIS

Illinois Minigrant Program
ACTION
175 West Jackson Blvd.,
Suite 1207
Chicago, IL 60604
(312) 353-3622

Description: Funding to establish local community projects, such as day-care centers, that encourage volunteerism; monies awarded must be matched by volunteer participation
$ Given: $500 to $10,000 per award
Requirements: Project volunteers must participate 1/2 hour for every dollar awarded
Contact: James Braxton

INDIANA

Indiana Minigrant Program
ACTION
46 East Ohio Street,
Room 457
Indianapolis, IN 46204
(317) 226-6724

Description: Funding to establish local community projects, such as day-care centers, that encourage volunteerism; monies awarded must be matched by volunteer participation
$ Given: $500 to $10,000 per award
Requirements: Project volunteers must participate 1/2 hour for every dollar awarded
Contact: Thomas Haskett

IOWA

Iowa Minigrant Program
ACTION
210 Walnut Street,
Room 722
Des Moines, IA 50309
(515) 284-4817

Description: Funding to establish local community projects, such as day-care centers, that encourage volunteerism; monies awarded must be matched by volunteer participation
$ Given: $500 to $10,000 per award
Requirements: Project volunteers must participate 1/2 hour for every dollar awarded
Contact: Joel Weinstein

KANSAS

Kansas Minigrant Program
ACTION
444 SE Quincy, Room 248
Topeka, KS 66603
(913) 295-2540

Description: Funding to establish local community projects, such as day-care centers, that encourage volunteerism; monies awarded must be matched by volunteer participation
$ Given: $500 to $10,000 per award
Requirements: Project volunteers must participate 1/2 hour for every dollar awarded
Contact: James M. Byrnes

KENTUCKY

Kentucky Minigrant Program
ACTION
Federal Building,
Room 372-D
600 Federal Place
Louisville, KY 40202
(502) 582-6384

Description: Funding to establish local community projects, such as day-care centers, that encourage volunteerism; monies awarded must be matched by volunteer participation
$ Given: $500 to $10,000 per award
Requirements: Project volunteers must participate 1/2 hour for every dollar awarded
Contact: Betsey Irvin Walls

LOUISIANA

Louisiana Minigrant Program
ACTION
626 Main Street, Suite 102
Baton Rouge, LA 70801
(504) 389-0471

Description: Funding to establish local community projects, such as day-care centers, that encourage volunteerism; monies awarded must be matched by volunteer participation
$ Given: $500 to $10,000 per award
Requirements: Project volunteers must participate 1/2 hour for every dollar awarded
Contact: Willard Labrie

VOLUNTEER PROGRAM FUNDING

MAINE

Maine Minigrant Program
ACTION
United States Courthouse
76 Pearl Street, Room 305
Portland, ME 04101
(207) 780-3414

Description: Funding to establish local community projects, such as day-care centers, that encourage volunteerism; monies awarded must be matched by volunteer participation
$ Given: $500 to $10,000 per award
Requirements: Project volunteers must participate 1/2 hour for every dollar awarded
Contact: Thomas Endres

MARYLAND

Maryland Minigrant Program
ACTION
31 Hopkins Plaza, Rm. 1125
Baltimore, MD 21201
(301) 962-4443

Description: Funding to establish local community projects, such as day-care centers, that encourage volunteerism; monies awarded must be matched by volunteer participation
$ Given: $500 to $10,000 per award
Requirements: Project volunteers must participate 1/2 hour for every dollar awarded
Contact: Jerry Yates

MASSACHUSETTS

Massachusetts Minigrant Program
ACTION
10 Causeway Street, Rm. 473
Boston, MA 02222
(617) 565-7015

Description: Funding to establish local community projects, such as day-care centers, that encourage volunteerism; monies awarded must be matched by volunteer participation
$ Given: $500 to $10,000 per award
Requirements: Project volunteers must participate 1/2 hour for every dollar awarded
Contact: Mal Coles

· ·

MICHIGAN

Michigan Minigrant Program
ACTION
231 West Lafayette
Boulevard, Room 658
Detroit, MI 48226
(313) 226-7848

Description: Funding to establish local community projects, such as day-care centers, that encourage volunteerism; monies awarded must be matched by volunteer participation
$ Given: $500 to $10,000 per award
Requirements: Project volunteers must participate 1/2 hour for every dollar awarded
Contact: Stan Stewart

MINNESOTA

Minnesota Minigrant Program
ACTION
431 South 7th Street,
Suite 2480
Minneapolis, MN 55401
(612) 334-4083

Description: Funding to establish local community projects, such as day-care centers, that encourage volunteerism; monies awarded must be matched by volunteer participation
$ Given: $500 to $10,000 per award
Requirements: Project volunteers must participate 1/2 hour for every dollar awarded
Contact: Robert Jackson

MISSISSIPPI

Mississippi Minigrant Program
ACTION
100 West Capital Street,
Room 1005A
Jackson, MS 39269
(605) 965-5664

Description: Funding to establish local community projects, such as day-care centers, that encourage volunteerism; monies awarded must be matched by volunteer participation
$ Given: $500 to $10,000 per award
Requirements: Project volunteers must participate 1/2 hour for every dollar awarded
Contact: Arthur Brown III

VOLUNTEER PROGRAM FUNDING

. . . .

MISSOURI

Missouri Minigrant Program
ACTION
911 Walnut, Room 1701
Kansas City, MO 64106
(816) 426-5256

Description: Funding to establish local community projects, such as day-care centers, that encourage volunteerism; monies awarded must be matched by volunteer participation
$ Given: $500 to $10,000 per award
Requirements: Project volunteers must participate 1/2 hour for every dollar awarded
Contact: John McDonald

MONTANA

Montana Minigrant Program
ACTION
301 South Park, Room 192
Helena, MT 59626
(406) 449-5404

Description: Funding to establish local community projects, such as day-care centers, that encourage volunteerism; monies awarded must be matched by volunteer participation
$ Given: $500 to $10,000 per award
Requirements: Project volunteers must participate 1/2 hour for every dollar awarded
Contact: Joe Lovelady

NEBRASKA

Nebraska Minigrant Program
ACTION
100 Centennial Mall, Room 293
Lincoln, NE 68508
(402) 437-5493

Description: Funding to establish local community projects, such as day-care centers, that encourage volunteerism; monies awarded must be matched by volunteer participation
$ Given: $500 to $10,000 per award
Requirements: Project volunteers must participate 1/2 hour for every dollar awarded
Contact: Anne Johnson

NEVADA

Nevada Minigrant Program
ACTION
4600 Kietzke Lane,
Suite E141
Reno, NV 89502
(702) 784-5314

Description: Funding to establish local community projects, such as day-care centers, that encourage volunteerism; monies awarded must be matched by volunteer participation
$ Given: $500 to $10,000 per award
Requirements: Project volunteers must participate 1/2 hour for every dollar awarded
Contact: Steven Gordon

NEW HAMPSHIRE

New Hampshire Minigrant Program
ACTION
Federal Post Office and
Courthouse
55 Pleasant Street, Rm. 316
Concord, NH 03301
(603) 225-1450

Description: Funding to establish local community projects, such as day-care centers, that encourage volunteerism; monies awarded must be matched by volunteer participation
$ Given: $500 to $10,000 per award
Requirements: Project volunteers must participate 1/2 hour for every dollar awarded
Contact: Peter Bender

NEW JERSEY

New Jersey Minigrant Program
ACTION
402 East State Street
Trenton, NJ 08608
(609) 989-2243

Description: Funding to establish local community projects, such as day-care centers, that encourage volunteerism; monies awarded must be matched by volunteer participation
$ Given: $500 to $10,000 per award
Requirements: Project volunteers must participate 1/2 hour for every dollar awarded
Contact: Stanley Gorland

VOLUNTEER PROGRAM FUNDING

. . . .

NEW MEXICO

**New Mexico Minigrant
Program**
ACTION
125 Lincoln Avenue,
Suite 214 B
Santa Fe, NM 87501
(505) 988-6577

Description: Funding to establish local community projects, such as day-care centers, that encourage volunteerism; monies awarded must be matched by volunteer participation
$ Given: $500 to $10,000 per award
Requirements: Project volunteers must participate 1/2 hour for every dollar awarded
Contact: Ernesto Ramos

NEW YORK

**New York Minigrant
Program**
ACTION
United States Courthouse
and Federal Building
445 Broadway, Room 103
Albany, NY 12207
(518) 472-3664

Description: Funding to establish local community projects, such as day-care centers, that encourage volunteerism; monies awarded must be matched by volunteer participation
$ Given: $500 to $10,000 per award
Requirements: Project volunteers must participate 1/2 hour for every dollar awarded
Contact: Carolyn Whitlock

NORTH CAROLINA

**North Carolina Minigrant
Program**
ACTION
300 Fayetteville Street Mall,
Room 131
Raleigh, NC 27601
(919) 856-4731

Description: Funding to establish local community projects, such as day-care centers, that encourage volunteerism; monies awarded must be matched by volunteer participation
$ Given: $500 to $10,000 per award
Requirements: Project volunteers must participate 1/2 hour for every dollar awarded
Contact: Robert Winston

NORTH DAKOTA

North Dakota Minigrant Program
ACTION
225 South Pierre Street,
Room 213
Pierre, SD 57501
(605) 224-5996

Description: Funding to establish local community projects, such as day-care centers, that encourage volunteerism; monies awarded must be matched by volunteer participation
$ Given: $500 to $10,000 per award
Requirements: Project volunteers must participate 1/2 hour for every dollar awarded
Contact: John Pohlman

OHIO

Ohio Minigrant Program
ACTION
Leveque Tower, 304-A
50 West Broad Street
Columbus, Ohio 43215
(614) 469-7441

Description: Funding to establish local community projects, such as day-care centers, that encourage volunteerism; monies awarded must be matched by volunteer participation
$ Given: $500 to $10,000 per award
Requirements: Project volunteers must participate 1/2 hour for every dollar awarded
Contact: Paul Schrader

OKLAHOMA

Oklahoma Minigrant Program
ACTION
200 NW 5th Street,
Suite 912
Oklahoma City, OK 73102
(405) 231-5201

Description: Funding to establish local community projects, such as day-care centers, that encourage volunteerism; monies awarded must be matched by volunteer participation
$ Given: $500 to $10,000 per award
Requirements: Project volunteers must participate 1/2 hour for every dollar awarded
Contact: Zeke Rodriquez

VOLUNTEER PROGRAM FUNDING

. . . .

OREGON

Oregon Minigrant Program
ACTION
511 NW Broadway,
Room 647
Portland, OR 97209
(503) 326-2261

Description: Funding to establish local community projects, such as day-care centers, that encourage volunteerism; monies awarded must be matched by volunteer participation
$ Given: $500 to $10,000 per award
Requirements: Project volunteers must participate 1/2 hour for every dollar awarded
Contact: Maureen Palma

PENNSYLVANIA

Pennsylvania Minigrant Program
ACTION
United States Customs House, Room 108
2nd and Chestnut Streets
Philadelphia, PA 19106
(215) 597-3543

Description: Funding to establish local community projects, such as day-care centers, that encourage volunteerism; monies awarded must be matched by volunteer participation
$ Given: $500 to $10,000 per award
Requirements: Project volunteers must participate 1/2 hour for every dollar awarded
Contact: Jorina Ahmed

RHODE ISLAND

Rhode Island Minigrant Program
ACTION
232 Pastore Building
Two Exchange Terrace
Providence, RI 02903
(401) 528-5424

Description: Funding to establish local community projects, such as day-care centers, that encourage volunteerism; monies awarded must be matched by volunteer participation
$ Given: $500 to $10,000 per award
Requirements: Project volunteers must participate 1/2 hour for every dollar awarded
Contact: Vincent Marzullo

. . . .

SOUTH CAROLINA

South Carolina Minigrant Program
ACTION
1835 Assembly Street, Room 872
Columbia, SC 29201
(803) 765-5771

Description: Funding to establish local community projects, such as day-care centers, that encourage volunteerism; monies awarded must be matched by volunteer participation
$ Given: $500 to $10,000 per award
Requirements: Project volunteers must participate 1/2 hour for every dollar awarded
Contact: Jerome J. Davis

SOUTH DAKOTA

South Dakota Minigrant Program
ACTION
225 South Pierre Street, Room 213
Pierre, SD 57501
(605) 224-5996

Description: Funding to establish local community projects, such as day-care centers, that encourage volunteerism; monies awarded must be matched by volunteer participation
$ Given: $500 to $10,000 per award
Requirements: Project volunteers must participate 1/2 hour for every dollar awarded
Contact: John Pohlman

TENNESSEE

Tennessee Minigrant Program
ACTION
265 Cumberland Bend Dr.
Nashville, TN 37228
(615) 736-5561

Description: Funding to establish local community projects, such as day-care centers, that encourage volunteerism; monies awarded must be matched by volunteer participation
$ Given: $500 to $10,000 per award
Requirements: Project volunteers must participate 1/2 hour for every dollar awarded
Contact: Alfred E. Johnson

VOLUNTEER PROGRAM FUNDING

• • • • • • • • • • • • • • • • • • •

TEXAS

Texas Minigrant Program
ACTION
611 East 6th Street,
Suite 107
Austin, TX 78701
(512) 482-5671

Description: Funding to establish local community projects, such as day-care centers, that encourage volunteerism; monies awarded must be matched by volunteer participation
$ Given: $500 to $10,000 per award
Requirements: Project volunteers must participate 1/2 hour for every dollar awarded
Contact: Jerry G. Thompson

UTAH

Utah Minigrant Program
ACTION
350 South Main Street,
Room 484
Salt Lake City, UT 84101
(801) 524-5411

Description: Funding to establish local community projects, such as day-care centers, that encourage volunteerism; monies awarded must be matched by volunteer participation
$ Given: $500 to $10,000 per award
Requirements: Project volunteers must participate 1/2 hour for every dollar awarded
Contact: Gary O'Neal

VERMONT

Vermont Minigrant Program
ACTION
Federal Post Office and
Courthouse
55 Pleasant Street,
Room 316
Concord, NH 03301
(603) 225-1450

Description: Funding to establish local community projects, such as day-care centers, that encourage volunteerism; monies awarded must be matched by volunteer participation
$ Given: $500 to $10,000 per award
Requirements: Project volunteers must participate 1/2 hour for every dollar awarded
Contact: Peter Bender

VIRGINIA

**Virginia Minigrant
Program**
ACTION
400 North 8th Street,
Room 1119
Richmond, VA 23240
(804) 771-2197

Description: Funding to establish local community projects, such as day-care centers, that encourage volunteerism; monies awarded must be matched by volunteer participation
$ Given: $500 to $10,000 per award
Requirements: Project volunteers must participate 1/2 hour for every dollar awarded
Contact: Lindsay Scott

WASHINGTON

**Washington Minigrant
Program**
ACTION
909 First Avenue,
Suite 3039
Seattle, WA 98174
(206) 442-4975

Description: Funding to establish local community projects, such as day-care centers, that encourage volunteerism; monies awarded must be matched by volunteer participation
$ Given: $500 to $10,000 per award
Requirements: Project volunteers must participate 1/2 hour for every dollar awarded
Contact: John Miller

WEST VIRGINIA

**West Virginia Minigrant
Program**
ACTION
603 Morris Street,
2nd Floor
Charleston, WV 25301
(304) 347-5246

Description: Funding to establish local community projects, such as day-care centers, that encourage volunteerism; monies awarded must be matched by volunteer participation
$ Given: $500 to $10,000 per award
Requirements: Project volunteers must participate 1/2 hour for every dollar awarded
Contact: Jean Taylor-Brown

. . . .

WISCONSIN

**Wisconsin Minigrant
Program**
ACTION
517 East Wisconsin Avenue,
Room 601
Milwaukee, WI 53202
(414) 291-1118

Description: Funding to establish local community
projects, such as day-care centers, that encourage
volunteerism; monies awarded must be matched by
volunteer participation
$ Given: $500 to $10,000 per award
Requirements: Project volunteers must participate 1/2
hour for every dollar awarded
Contact: Michael Murphy

Index

C

California Minigrant Program, CA, 193
California Native American Training Programs, CA, 11
Campbell Soup Co., NJ, 151
Capitol Hill Hospital, DC, 106
Cardiac Pacemaker, MN, 141
Cardinal Glennon Children's Hospital, MO, 144
Carpenter Technology Corporation, PA, 170
Carraway Hospital, AL, 87
Carver Corp., WA, 186
Catherine McAuley Health System, MI, 139
Cedars of Lebanon Hospital, FL, 109
Center for Children & Youth, NE, 73
Centinela Hospital, CA, 91
Central Main Medical Center, ME, 131
Certified Grocers of Florida, FL, 109
Champion International, CT, 103
Charleston Area Medical Center, WV, 188
Charo Los Angeles City Hall So. Child Development Center, CA, 2
Chemical Bank, NY, 155
Child and Family Services, CA, 2
Child Protection Services, ND, 75
Child Protection Services, SD, 78
Child Protective Services Division, RI, 77
Child Protective Services Section, AZ, 66
Child Protective Services, TN, 78
Child Welfare & Protective Services, Guam, 82
Child Welfare Services, OK, 76
Child Welfare/Social Services Division, IN, 70
Children & Youth Family Services Division, ND, 75
Children in Need of Care, KS, 70
Children's Hospital and Health Center, San Diego, CA, 92
Children's Hospital Medical Center, Dayton, OH, 164
Children's Hospital, Los Angeles, CA, 92
Children's Hospital, MA, 134
Children's Hospital, MN, 141
Children's Hospital, NE, 148
Children's Services Division, OR, 77
Children, Youth & Families Program Office, FL, 68
Chomerics, MA, 134
Christian Hospital Northeast/Northwest, MO, 144
CIGNA Co., CT, 103
Circle K Corp., AZ, 88 .
Citibank, NY, 156
Cleveland Clinic, OH, 164
CMP Publications, NY, 156
Colonial Penn Service Corp., PA, 170
Colorado Minigrant Program, CO, 193
Colorado Native American Training Programs, CO, 11
Columbus Hospital, MT, 147
Commerce Clearing House, Inc., CA, 92
Commission on Children & Youth, TN, 78
Community Hospital of Roanoke, VA, 184
Community Methodist Hospital, KY, 128
Compaq Computer Corp., TX, 179
Con Edison, NY, 156
Conant Associates, UT, 183
Concord Hospital, NH, 150
Connecticut Minigrant Program, CT, 193
Connecticut Valley Hospital, CT, 103
Connections for Children, CA, 2
Copley Memorial Hospital, IL, 119
Corning, NY, 156
Cox Enterprises, GA, 115

Crystal Stairs, Inc., CA, 2
Current, Inc., CO, 101
Cushing Hospital, MA, 135

D

Dalton & Lightfoot Development Corp., FL, 109
Dana Farber Cancer Institite, MA, 134
Dataproducts Corp., CA, 92
Deaconess Hospital, MO, 144
Deaconess Hospital, WA, 187
Dede Wallace Institute, TN, 176
Dekalb Medical Center, GA, 115
Delaware Minigrant Program, DE, 193
Department for Children & Their Families, RI, 77
Department of Children & Family Services, IL, 69
Department of Children & Youth Services, CT, 68
Department of Family Services, MT, 73
Department of Human Resources, American Samoa, 81
Department of Human Services, OH, 76
Department of Public Welfare, MS, 72
Department of Social Services, Puerto Rico, 82
Digital Equipment, MA, 135
Division of Child & Family Services, ME, 71
Division of Child Protective Services, DE, 68
Division of Child Welfare Services, CO, 67
Division of Children & Family Services, AR, 67
Division of Children & Family Services, WA, 80
Division of Children Services, MN, 72
Division of Children, Youth & Family Services, LA, 71
Division of Children, Youth & Family, Virgin Islands, 83
Division of Family & Children's Services, AL, 66
Division of Family & Youth Services, AK, 66
Division of Family Services, KY, 70
Division of Family Services, MO, 72
Division of Family Services, UT, 79
Division of Family Support, AZ, 66
Division of Social Services, American Samoa, 81
Division of Social Services, VT, 79
Division of Youth & Family Services, NJ, 74
Doctor's Hospital, LA, 129
Dominion Bankshares, VA, 184
Kevin F. Donohoe Co., The, PA, 170
Dow Chemical, MI, 139
Doylestown Hospital, PA, 170
Dr. Pepper – 7-Up Companies, TX, 179
Dravo, PA, 170
Duda, A. & Sons, Inc., FL, 109
DuPont, DE, 105

E

Early Childhood Services/Family-Based Services, ND, 75
East Jefferson General Hospital, LA, 130
East Orange General Hospital, NJ, 151
Eastman Kodak Company, NY, 156
Edgewater Hospital, IL, 119
Educational Testing Service, NJ, 151
Elliot Hospital, NH, 150

F

Family & Children Services Branch, CA, 67
Family & Children's Services Operations Office, NY, 74
Family Services Administration, DC, 68
Farm Bureau Insurance, FL, 109
Federal Reserve Bank, GA, 115
Fel-Pro, IL, 120
First Atlanta Corp., GA, 115

Books in Laurie Blum's **Free Money** Series

. . . .

THE FREE MONEY FOR CHILD CARE SERIES

Free Money for Day Care
- Advice on finding financial aid for family day care, child care centers, in-house care, and camp and summer programs

Free Money for Private Schools
- Where to find money for preschool and nursery education, private primary schools, and private secondary schools

Free Money for Children's Medical and Dental Care
- Ways to receive money for both long- and short-term medical care, dental and orthodontic treatment, and dermatological procedures

Free Money for Behavioral and Genetic Childhood Disorders
- Free Money for treatment of learning disabilities, eating disorders, retardation, alcohol and drug abuse, neurological disturbances, and sleep disorders

THE FREE MONEY FOR HEALTH CARE SERIES

Free Money for Diseases of Aging
- Find money to help pay for major surgery and medical care for diseases of aging such as Alzheimer's, Parkinson's, stroke, and other chronic illnesses

Free Money for Heart Disease and Cancer Care
- Ways to receive money for the diagnosis and treatment (surgery or long-term care) of cancer and heart disease

Free Money for Fertility Treatments
- Where to look for Free Money for infertility testing, treatment, insemination, and preliminary adoption expenses

Free Money for the Care and Treatment of Mental and Emotional Disorders
- Detailed guidance on locating Free Money for psychological care